Lecture Notes of the Institute for Computer Sciences, Social Informatics and Telecommunications Engineering   **434**

More information about this series at https://link.springer.com/bookseries/8197

Shuiguang Deng · Albert Zomaya ·
Ning Li (Eds.)

Mobile Computing, Applications, and Services

12th EAI International Conference, MobiCASE 2021
Virtual Event, November 13–14, 2021
Proceedings

 Springer

Editors
Shuiguang Deng
Zhejiang University
Hangzhou, China

Albert Zomaya
University of Sydney
Sydney, NSW, Australia

Ning Li
Beijing Information Science
and Technology University
Beijing, China

ISSN 1867-8211   ISSN 1867-822X (electronic)
Lecture Notes of the Institute for Computer Sciences, Social Informatics
and Telecommunications Engineering
ISBN 978-3-030-99202-6   ISBN 978-3-030-99203-3 (eBook)
https://doi.org/10.1007/978-3-030-99203-3

This Springer imprint is published by the registered company Springer Nature Switzerland AG
The registered company address is: Gewerbestrasse 11, 6330 Cham, Switzerland

Preface

We are delighted to introduce the proceedings of the 12th European Alliance for Innovation (EAI) International Conference on Mobile Computing, Applications and Services (MobiCASE). This conference brought together researchers, developers, and practitioners around the world who are interested in mobile computing and leveraging or developing mobile services, applications, and technologies that improve the mobile ecosystem.

The technical program of MobiCASE 2021 consisted of nine full papers which were selected from 21 paper submissions. The conference tracks were as follows: Track 1 - Mobile Application and Deep Learning and Track 2 - Mobile Application with Data Analysis. Aside from the high-quality technical paper presentations, the technical program also featured a keynote speech about "Online Intelligence at Edge: Theory and Implementation" given by Haisheng Tan from the University of Science and Technology of China.

Coordination with the steering chair, Imrich Chlamtac, and steering committee members was essential for the success of the conference. We sincerely appreciate their constant support and guidance. It was also a great pleasure to work with such an excellent organizing committee team for their hard work in organizing and supporting the conference. In particular, we are grateful to the Technical Program Committee who completed the peer-review process for the technical papers and helped to put together a high-quality technical program. We are also grateful to Conference Manager Lucia Sladeckova for her support and all the authors who submitted their papers to the MobiCASE 2021 conference.

We strongly believe that the MobiCASE conference provides a good forum for all researchers, developers, and practitioners to discuss all science and technology aspects that are relevant to mobile computing, applications, and services. We also expect that the future MobiCASE conferences will be as successful and stimulating as this year's, as indicated by the contributions presented in this volume.

November 2021

Shuiguang Deng
Albert Zomaya
Ning Li
Javid Taheri
Shangguang Wang
Honghao Gao
Jun Yu

Organization

Steering Committee

Chair

Imrich Chlamtac   University of Trento, Italy

Members

Thomas Phan   Cruise, USA
Petros Zerfos   IBM Research, USA

Organizing Committee

General Chairs

Shuiguang Deng   Zhejiang University, China
Albert Zomaya   University of Sydney, Australia
Ning Li   Beijing Information Science and Technology
                              University, China

Technical Program Committee Chairs

Javid Taheri   Karlstad University, Sweden
Shangguang Wang   Beijing University of Posts and Telecommunications,
                              China
Honghao Gao   Shanghai University, China
Jun Yu   Hangzhou Dianzi University, China

Local Chairs

Yuyu Yin   Hangzhou Dianzi University, China
You Xindong   Beijing Information Science and Technology
                              University, China

Workshops Chairs

Yuyu Yin   Hangzhou Dianzi University, China
Ramón J. Durán Barroso   Universidad de Valladolid, Spain

Publicity and Social Media Chair

Hongyue Wu   Tianjin University, China

Sponsorship and Exhibits Chair

Honghao Gao   Shanghai University, China

Publications Chair

Youhuizi Li   Hangzhou Dianzi University, China

Web Chair

Zhengzhe Xiang   Zhejiang University, China

Conference Manager

Barbora Cintava   EAI, Slovakia

Technical Program Committee

Bin Cao	Zhejiang University of Technology, China
Buqing Cao	Hunan University of Science and Technology, China
Congfeng Jiang	Hangzhou Dianzi University, China
Dongjing Wang	Hangzhou Dianzi University, China
Yucong Duan	Hainan University, China
Guobing Zou	Shanghai University, China
Jiwei Huang	Beijing University of Posts and Telecommunications, China
Youhuizi Li	Hangzhou Dianzi University, China
Junhao Wen	Chongqing University, China
Jian Wang	Wuhan University, China
Yanmei Zhang	Central University of Finance and Economics, China
Jiuyun Xu	China University of Petroleum, China
Li Kuang	Central South University, China
Shunmei Meng	Nanjing University of Science and Technology, China
Kai Peng	Beijing University of Posts and Telecommunications, China
Shizhan Chen	Tianjin University, China
Xiaobing Sun	Yangzhou University, China
Yunni Xia	Chongqing University, China
Xiaolong Xu	Nanjing University of Science and Technology, China
Yihai Chen	Shanghai University, China
Yuyu Yin	Hangzhou Dianzi University, China
Yiping Wen	Hunan University of Science and Technology, China
Yueshen Xu	Xidian University, China
Yutao Ma	Wuhan University, China
Jun Zeng	Chongqing University, China
Yiwen Zhang	Anhui University, China
Zijian Zhang	Beijing Institute of Technology, China
Zhongqin Bi	Shanghai University of Electric Power, China
Wang Haiyan	Nanjing University of Posts and Telecommunications, China
Luiz F. Bittencourt	University of Campinas, Brazil
Abid Hussain	Career Point University, India

Armando Ruggeri   University of Messina, Italy
Javid Taheri   Karlstad University, Sweden
Antonino Galletta   University of Messina, Italy
Massimo Villari   University of Messina, Italy
Eirini Eleni Tsiropoulou   University of New Mexico, USA
Edelberto Franco   Federal University of Juiz de Fora, Brazil
Mario Colosi   University of Messina, Italy
Christian Sicari   University of Insubria, Italy
Giuseppe Di Modica   University of Bologna, Italy
Auday Al-Dulaimy   Malardalen University, Sweden

Contents

Mobile Application and Deep Learning

YOLO-RFB: An Improved Traffic Sign Detection Model

Zhongqin Bi[1], Fuqiang Xu[1], Meijing Shan[2(✉)], and Ling Yu[1]

[1] School of Computer Science and Technology, Shanghai University of Electric Power,
Shanghai 200090, China
[2] Department of Information Science and Technology, East China University of Political
Science and Law, Shanghai 201620, China
5805831@qq.com

Abstract. With the development of intelligent transportation system, the detection method of traffic signs plays an important role in unmanned driving. However, due to the real-time and reliability characteristics of the automatic driving system, each traffic sign needs to be processed in a specific time interval to ensure the precision of the test results. Automatic driving is developing rapidly and has made great progress. Various traffic sign detection algorithms are proposed. Especially, convolutional neural network algorithm is concerned because of its fast execution and high recognition rate. But in the real world of complex traffic conditions, those algorithms still have problems such as poor real-time detection, low precision, false detection and high missed detection rate. To overcome those problems, this paper proposed an improved algorithm named as YOLO-RFB based on YOLO V4 network. Based on YOLO V4 network, the main feature extraction network is pruned, and convolution layer is replaced by RFB structure in two output feature layers. In the detection results of GTSDB data sets, the mAP of improved algorithm achieves 85.59%, 4.76% points higher than the original algorithm, and the FPS reaches 48.72, which is slightly lower than that of the original YOLO V4 algorithm 50.21.

Keywords: Unmanned driving · Traffic sign detection · GTSDB · YOLO V4

1 Introduction

In recent years, with the application of deep learning technology in the field of unmanned driving, the commercialization of unmanned vehicles has gradually become the focus and trend. Car companies and Internet companies are rushing to enter the self-driving field. The automobile industry is a special industry, because it involves the safety of passengers, any accident is unacceptable, so there are almost strict requirements for safety and reliability. Therefore, in the process of studying unmanned driving, the precision, real-time performance and robustness of the algorithm are highly required [1]. Traffic

© ICST Institute for Computer Sciences, Social Informatics and Telecommunications Engineering 2022
Published by Springer Nature Switzerland AG 2022. All Rights Reserved
S. Deng et al. (Eds.): MobiCASE 2021, LNICST 434, pp. 3–18, 2022.
https://doi.org/10.1007/978-3-030-99203-3_1

sign detection is one of the important parts of unmanned driving system, which plays an important role in reducing safety accidents and assisting drivers in driving. Due to the high requirement of real-time detection of traffic signs in the process of vehicle driving, and the influence of light, weather and shooting Angle, it is difficult to detect traffic signs in real time. In addition, due to the large number of traffic signs in the image, the small target, the pixel value contains few features, which increases the difficulty of traffic sign detection. Currently, there are four main detection methods for traffic signs, which are color-based method, shape-based method, multi-feature fusion based method and deep learning based method [2]. Among them, the detection method based on color is susceptible to the influence of illumination and other factors, and its robustness is poor under complex illumination conditions. The factors such as color difference and complex background will also cause the loss of effective information. The shape-based detection method has good robustness and strong anti-noise ability. However, due to the large amount of computation and high requirements on hardware, it cannot meet the requirements of real-time performance. The methods based on multi-feature fusion often need to extract target features manually. The traffic sign detection method based on deep learning can automatically extract target features and has good model generalization ability, which has been widely used.

In this paper, on the basis of analyzing the problems existing in the application of YOLO V4 network in traffic sign detection, the optimized YOLO V4 network can not only quickly classify traffic signs, but also effectively improve the precision of traffic sign detection. Firstly, this paper pruned the backbone network in YOLO V4 network to reduce convolution operations and effectively improve the speed of the model without losing too much performance. Secondly, a new module is added to the network to enhance the feature extraction ability of the network by simulating human receptive field.

2   YOLO V4

As shown in Fig. 1, the network of YOLO V4 [3] consists of three parts: trunk network, neck network and head network. Among them, the backbone network is CSPDarkNet53, CSP [4] network is a new backbone network that can enhance the learning ability of neural networks, and maintain precision, reduce computing bottlenecks and memory costs while being lightweight. Darknet53 is the backbone network used by YOLOv3 [14], which combines the ideas of CSP network to form the CSPDarkNet53 network. The neck network was SPP [5] and PAN [6]. SPP network is the same size of features obtained by convolution of CSPDarknet53. PAN network has the structure of repeated feature extraction, which improves the precision of small object detection. The head network is responsible for the final prediction task.

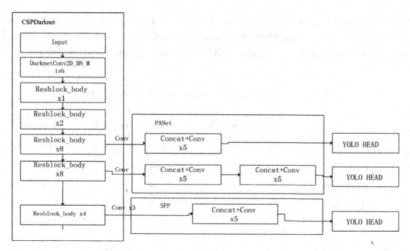

Fig. 1. Network structure of YOLO V4

3 Improved YOLO V4

In this paper, the backbone network and feature extraction network are improved based on YOLO V4 network model.

3.1 RFB

RFB [8] network is used for object detection, which can achieve good results while taking into account speed. This network mainly introduces Receptive Field Block (RFB) into SSD [15] network. The purpose of introducing RFB is to enhance the feature extraction capability of the network by simulating the Receptive Field of human vision. In terms of structure, RFB draw on the idea of Inception Mainly, dilated convolution [17] is added on the basis of Inception to effectively increase the receptive field. The overall improvement is based on SSD network to improve the detection speed while ensuring the precision.

RFB introduced the concept of initial frame, that is in the center of the cell of each characteristic graph set a series of scales and different initial box size, they will reverse mapping to one of the original position, if the initial frame's position at the right moment and the location of the true target box overlap degree is high, then predict the initial frame's category by loss function and fine-tune the shape of these initial boxes to make it match the actual target box of the tag [18].

The initial box has two main parameters: scale S and aspect ratio a. Assuming that m feature graphs are used for prediction [20], the initial box calculation formula of each feature graph is as follows:

$$S_k = S_{\min} + \frac{S_{\max} - S_{\min}}{m - 1}(k - 1), k \in [1, m] \tag{1}$$

With the deepening of network layers (smaller feature graphs), the scale of initial frames increases linearly. The minimum initial box scale is 0.2, and the maximum is 0.9. It is the general scale design principle of RFB. The details are shown in Table 1.

Table 1. The default boxes size on each feature map

Index	Feature map	Feature map size	Default box scale	True size
1	Conv4_3	38	0.2	60
2	Conv7	19	0.34	102
3	RFB stride 2	10	0.48	144
4	RFB stride 2	5	0.62	186
5	Conv10_2	3	0.76	228
6	Conv11_2	1	0.9	270

The width to height ratio of the initial box is set as follows:

$$a_r \in \{1, 2, 3, \frac{1}{2}, \frac{1}{3}\} \tag{2}$$

The initial frame width and height on each feature graph can be obtained by the following formula:

$$w_k^a = S_k \sqrt{a_r} \tag{3}$$

$$h_k^a = \frac{S_k}{\sqrt{a_r}} \tag{4}$$

Added a square initial box for the initial box with an aspect ratio of 1:

$$S_k' = \sqrt{S_k + S_{k+1}} \tag{5}$$

The details of the feature map are shown in Table 2.

3.2 YOLO-RFB

YOLO V4 has higher detection precision than previous algorithms, but it will take a long time if the detection is carried out on the terminal with poor hardware performance. In order to improve the detection speed and precision of traffic signs, this section studies the YOLO V4 network and makes corresponding improvements [19].

The original YOLO V4 model replaced the trunk extraction network by DarkNet53 with CSPDarkNet53, using a CSPNet structure to enhance CNN's learning ability and maintain precision while being lightweight. At the output end, there are three characteristic layers of different sizes, P3, P4 and P5, whose sizes are 1/8, 1/16 and 1/32 of the original input size respectively. After a convolution operation, the feature images

Table 2. Characteristic graph and its size used in RFB network

Feature map	Size
Conv4_3	38 * 38
Conv7	19 * 19
RFB stride 2	10 * 10
RFB stride 2	5 * 5
Conv10_2	3 * 3
Conv11_2	1 * 1

output by the two feature layers P3 and P4 enter the PANet structure for feature fusion. Feature layer P5 needs to conduct a convolution operation, then enter SPP structure for maximum pooling, separate context features, conduct another convolution operation, and finally enter PANet structure for feature fusion. These operations enable the model to extract the features of different scales and types effectively to a certain extent [7].

In the actual scene, traffic sign images often occupy a small area of the image, and their appearance is also greatly affected by the environment. If the original YOLO V4 model is directly used for training and detection, the result is not ideal. And a large number of experimental analysis show that the number of large target samples is often more than small one in network model training, which leads to the lack of information obtained by network model in feature extraction of small target samples, and small targets cannot be fully trained. Therefore, the improvement of network model should start with how to strengthen the ability of network model to extract small target samples and increase the feature information.

In view of the fact that traffic signs are small size targets in images, as well as environmental factors, the ideas of YOLO V4 model are referenced and modified in this section to obtain the improved YOLO V4 network structure, YOLO-RFB, as shown in Fig. 2. The main aspects of improvement of YOLO V4 network are shown as follows:

- The CSPDarkNet53 trunk extraction network was pruned to reduce the number of Resblock_body in the three output feature layers from 8, 8, 4 to 2, 4, 4 respectively, and reduce part of the convolution operation to improve the speed effectively while the performance of the model is guaranteed as much as possible.
- The convolution operation required by P3 and P4 output feature layers is replaced with RFB structure. RFB adds a wormhole convolution layer to Inception to enhance the feature extraction capability of the network by simulating the receptive field of human vision, so as to obtain higher semantic level and more global feature information. In this way, the characteristic information of traffic signs, especially small target samples, can be better extracted in the training process, and the performance of the network model in traffic sign detection can be improved more effectively.

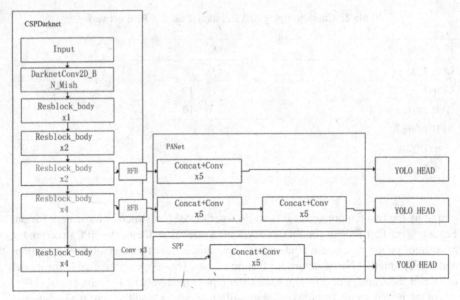

Fig. 2. Network structure of YOLO-RFB

4   Experiment and Analysis

Experiments are carried out on GTSDB data set to prove the effectiveness of the improved algorithm.

4.1   Common Data Sets

In the early 1990s, scholars from all over the world began to study traffic sign detection. But until 2011, the lack of publicly available traffic sign data sets was a major problem. In 2011, Traffic sign Detection and Recognition Competition was held in Germany, which was based on German Traffic Sign Benchmark Data Set (GTSBD) [9], indicating that traffic sign detection and recognition received high attention from the world. The proposed public benchmark data set makes the traffic sign detection algorithm has a unified evaluation standard, so as to compare the performance of the proposed network model or algorithm, also promotes the research progress of traffic sign detection and recognition.

GTSBD contains two data sets, German Traffic Sign Detection Benchmark (GTSDB) [10] and German Traffic Sign Recognition Benchmark (GTSRB) [11]. The GTSDB data set is used for the detection task of traffic signs, which contains 43 categories, which are divided into three categories in the detection task: For Prohibitory, Mandatory and Danger, a total of 900 images of driving scenes are available, and total of 852 traffic signs are available. The training set contains 396 samples of prohibitory traffic signs (59.5%), 114 samples of mandatory traffic signs (17.1%) and 156 samples of danger traffic signs (23.4%), and the test set contains 161 images of prohibitory traffic signs, 49 images of mandatory traffic signs and 63 images of danger traffic signs. Figure 3 shows a sample image from the GTSDB dataset.

Fig. 3. Sample image in GTSDB dataset

4.2 Experimental Environment and Hyperparameter Setting

The experiment is completed under Ubuntu16.04 operating system. The hardware used are as follows: CPU: Intel Core I9-10900K; GPU: NVIDIA GTX 3080 independent graphics card, 10G video memory. Python3.6 is the programming language used, and Pytorch1.7 is the development framework for deep learning.

The GTSDB dataset was used in the experiment (see Sect. 4.1 for details). Using the prior box of the original model cannot directly achieve the desired effect, since the GTSDB data set is much different from the COCO data set tested by the original YOLO V4. Therefore, k-means clustering method was used to obtain the prior boxes matching the GTSDB data set before the experiment.

Since the results of multiple experiments have little influence on the experimental results, Mosaic data enhancement and learning rate cosine annealing decay method are used instead of Label Smoothing. Before the training and detection of the improved YOLO V4 model, the original YOLO V4 model was first used to conduct experiments on the GTSDB data set, and the results were recorded as experimental comparison data. In the training process, the input size is set as 608 * 608, the batch size is 16, and the initial learning rate is 0.001. The optimizer uses Adam with step_size = 1 and gamma = 0.95. The total number of training steps (Epoch) was 400. In the first 200 steps, the learning rate dynamic decline method was used. Starting from the 201th step, the initial value of the learning rate was set as 1e−5. The cosine annealing attenuation method was used to change the learning rate, and the value of the minimum learning rate was set as 1e−8.

4.3 Evaluation Indicators

Mean Average Precision (mAP), Average Precision (AP), Precision and Recall are often used to evaluate the detection effect of the model in the field of object detection, Frames Per Second (FPS) and Giga Floating-point Operations Per Second (GigaFLOPS) were used to evaluate the detection performance.

Formula (6) and Formula (7) are the Precision and Recall calculation formulas. TP represents the input of the positive sample that the model thinks is positive, FP represents the input that the model misjudged as a positive sample, and FN represents the input that the model misjudged as a negative sample.

$$presicion = TP/(TP + FP) \tag{6}$$

$$recall = TP/(TP + FN) \tag{7}$$

A PR curve can be obtained by using Precision and Recall as horizontal and vertical coordinates, and the area under the PR curve is called AP index. The results of Precision and Recall are comprehensively evaluated. The definition is as follows:

$$AP_i = \sum_{k=1}^{N} p(k)\Delta r(k) \tag{8}$$

In Formula (8), $p(k)$ is the precision corresponding to the change point k of recall rate; $\Delta r(k)$ is the change of recall rate corresponding to change point K. N is the number of change points of recall rate; Different categories have different AP, i indicates the index of the category.

mAP averages the AP of all classes. The definition is as follows:

$$mAP = \frac{1}{m}\sum_{i=1}^{m} AP_i \tag{9}$$

The loss function is generally used to evaluate the error between the predicted value and the real of the model. It plays a key role in the speed of network learning and the final prediction effect of the model. IOU [12] is a commonly used indicator in object detection, used to reflect the detection effect between the prediction box and the target box. It is defined as:

$$IOU = \frac{|A \cap B|}{|A \cup B|} \tag{10}$$

YOLO V4 uses CIOU [13] to replace the regression loss function of the original BBOX. For object detection, it is necessary to encode the real frame after obtaining it and transform it into the form of prediction frame, and then compare the prediction result of the real frame with that of the network to optimize the network structure and make the prediction of the frame more accurate. CIOU is an improved version of IOU with the following formula:

$$CIOU = IOU - \frac{\rho^2(b, b^{gt})}{c^2} - \alpha v \tag{11}$$

Where, b and b^{gt} represent the central point of the prediction frame and the real frame respectively; ρ^2 is the Euclidean distance of two central points; c represents the diagonal distance of the smallest closure region that can contain both the prediction box and the real box. Among them:

$$\alpha = \frac{v}{1 - IOU + v} \tag{12}$$

$$v = \frac{4}{\pi^2}(\arctan \frac{w^{gt}}{h^{gt}} - \arctan \frac{w}{h})^2 \tag{13}$$

αv is positively correlated with the frame height difference between the real frame and the prediction frame. CIOU refers to the deviation degree between the real box and the prediction one, then the LOSS function is:

$$LOSS_{CIOU} = 1 - IOU + \frac{\rho^2(b, b^{gt})}{c^2} + \alpha v \tag{14}$$

In addition to detection precision, detection speed is another important index of the object detection model. Real-time detection can be realized only when the speed reaches a certain level. The current metric used to assess detection speed is FPS, which is the number of images that can be processed per second. Generally speaking, when the FPS of the model is greater than 30, it is considered that the model meets the standard of real-time monitoring [16].

4.4 Experimental Results and Comparative Presentation

Detection precision and speed are very important in traffic sign detection tasks since vehicles in the real world are usually running at high speed, the size and cost of the network model in the vehicle system should also be considered. Therefore, the precision, speed and Parameter of the detection model must be evaluated.

The dimension of prior box of the original YOLO V4 model is (12, 16), (19, 36), (40, 28), (36, 75), (76, 55), (72, 146), (142, 110), (192, 243), (459, 401). The dimension of this group of prior frames is obtained by K-means clustering for COCO data set, while the data set tested in this paper is GTSDB data set, so the dimension of prior frames needs to be determined again. Therefore, before the experiment, K-means clustering method was used to cluster the GTSDB data set to generate the dimensions of new prior frames and obtain the dimensions of nine prior frames. (9, 15), (10, 18), (12, 20), (13, 22), (14, 25), (17, 29), (20, 34), (27, 45), (40, 66).They were assigned to the three feature maps with different scales, and the smaller prior frames were assigned to the feature maps with larger scales.

The loss curves of training sets and test sets of the original YOLO V4 model and the improved YOLO V4 model during training are shown in Fig. 4. As can be seen from the figure, the fluctuation of loss function on the training set and test set of YOLO V4 model is particularly severe during training, while the fluctuation of the model proposed is relatively gentle and its curve drops faster, indicating that the improved model performs better in the training process. Because YOLO-RFB model uses RFB module according to the characteristics of traffic sign data set, which strengthens the semantic features of feature graph, thus improving the generalization ability of network, making network model very excellent in training effect.

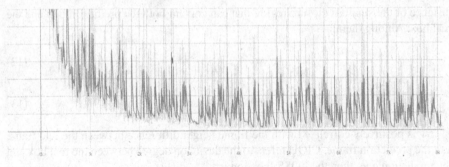

Loss curve of YOLO V4 model on training set

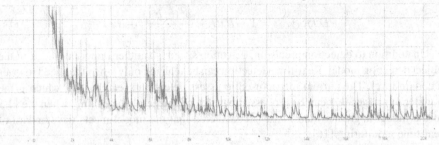

Loss curve of YOLO -RFB model on training set

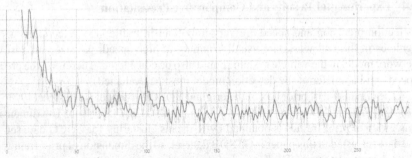

Loss curve of YOLO V4 model on test set

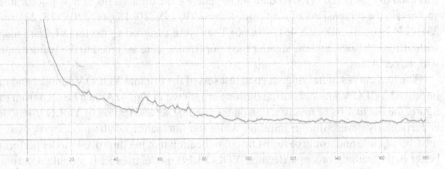

Loss curve of YOLO-RFB model on test set

Fig. 4. Comparison of loss curve between YOLO V4 and YOLO-RFB

Figure 5 shows the comparison of precision and recall curves (PR curves) of YOLO V4 model and YOLO-RFB in the GTSDB data set of three traffic signs. The PR curves of YOLO V4 model on three different traffic signs are shown on the left, and the PR curves of improved YOLO V4 model on three different traffic signs are shown on the right. The area formed by PR curve is the AP of the corresponding traffic sign type. The higher AP is, the better the detection performance is. As can be seen from the data in the figure, the improved YOLO V4 model has good detection performance, and the detection results of each type of traffic signs are superior to YOLO V4. Because the improved YOLO V4 model adds the RFB module to the original YOLO V4 feature output layer, which can enhance the feature extraction ability of the network by simulating the receptive field of human vision, obtain higher semantic level and more global feature information, and detect traffic sign information more effectively. Thus, the performance of network model in traffic sign detection task is improved.

Table 3 shows the detailed precision results of each traffic sign superclass, as well as the Precision, Recall and average precision (AP) obtained by each detection model. As can be seen from the test results in the table, the AP of mandatory traffic signs is the lowest in almost all model test results, while there are obvious differences among other types of APs. The prohibitory traffic signs achieved the best results in each model, reaching 99.37% in the Cascaded model. These results are related to the distribution of sample numbers in the GTSDB dataset (59.5% for prohibitory traffic signs and 17.1% for mandatory traffic signs). Compared with the traditional two-stage traffic sign detection model Faster R-CNN Resnet 50, YOLO-RFB model still has a certain gap in the detection of compulsory traffic signs. YOLO-RFB model has significantly improved the detection results of each superclass compared with the existing one-stage model. AP of prohibitory traffic signs has increased by more than 5% points, and AP of danger traffic signs has also been greatly improved.

Finally, the execution time of YOLO-RFB was compared with that of traditional detection methods. Table 4 shows the mAP, FPS, GFLOP and Parameter obtained by various detection models. According to the data in the table, the mAP of the two-stage detection model is significantly higher than that of the one-stage detection model, but its FPS is the lowest. This is because all the two-stage detection models are formed into a series of candidate boxes as samples, and then the samples are classified through the convolutional neural network. Automatic driving technology has high requirements for real-time detection, and the detection speed of two-stage model is often not up to the requirements. Although the mAP of the one-stage detection model is slightly lower, the FPS is all over 40, which can achieve a stable real-time detection effect. The original YOLO V4 model was a fast and accurate choice with a mAP of 80.83% and an FPS of 50.21. The performance of YOLO-RFB model in FPS is not significantly decreased, but the performance of mAP is greatly improved, it can be seen that the improved model has better performance, stronger robustness and better generalization ability.

As shown in Fig. 6, YOLO-RFB model is used to detect images of GTSDB data set. The left image is the detection result of YOLO-RFB model, and the right is the detection result of original YOLO V4 model. The score of visual detection is greater than the threshold of 0.3. These images show three common scenarios: the first is a normal driving scenario on the road, with an extra detection box on the right side of

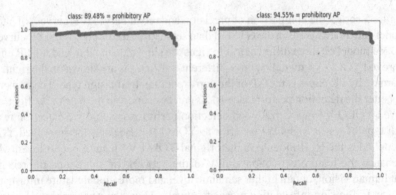

PR curves of YOLO V4 (left) and YOLO-RFB (right) on Prohibitory signs

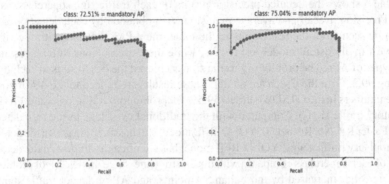

PR curves of YOLO V4 (left) and YOLO-RFB (right) on Mandatory signs

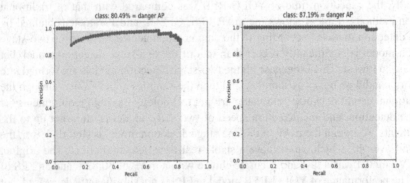

PR curves of YOLO V4 (left) and YOLO-RFB (right) on Danger Signs

Fig. 5. Performance comparison chart of YOLO V4 and YOLO-RFB

Table 3. The detection results of each traffic sign detection model on GTSDB

Model	Class	Precision (%)	Recall (%)	AP (%)
Faster R-CNN Resnet 50	Prohibitory	91.38	98.75	98.62
	Mandatory	70.00	85.71	85.15
	Danger	79.45	92.06	90.78
Cascaded R-CNN	Prohibitory	84.66	99.38	99.37
	Mandatory	76.67	93.88	92.58
	Danger	86.76	93.65	93.52
MST-TSD	Prohibitory	96.95	78.88	78.77
	Mandatory	90.00	55.10	54.46
	Danger	93.18	65.08	65.05
Yolov3	Prohibitory	92.31	89.44	88.73
	Mandatory	79.07	69.39	65.70
	Danger	94.55	82.54	82.06
YOLO V4	Prohibitory	88.02	91.30	89.48
	Mandatory	77.55	77.55	72.51
	Danger	88.14	82.54	80.49
YOLO-RFB	Prohibitory	89.53	95.43	94.55
	Mandatory	80.85	77.55	75.04
	Danger	98.21	87.30	87.19

Table 4. Performance of traffic sign detection models on GTSDB

Model	mAP (%)	FPS	GFLOP	Parameter (10^6)
Faster R-CNN Resnet 50	95.77	2.26	1837.54	59.41
Cascaded R-CNN	95.15	11.70	269.90	64.59
MST-TSD	66.10	42.12	7.59	13.47
Yolov3	78.83	46.55	62.78	50.59
YOLO V4	80.83	50.21	63.84	63.94
YOLO_RFB	85.59	48.72	81.06	71.89

the image, which mistakenly identifies the background building as a traffic sign, while the YOLO-RFB model does not detect; In the second scenario, driving on the street with multiple traffic signs of different categories, the model can only detect one traffic sign without improvement, while the improved model can well avoid the occurrence of missed detection. The third is the scenario with multiple traffic signs on both sides of the road. It can be observed that the unimproved model missed one traffic sign, while the improved model can detect all traffic signs well. From the comparison of detection results, it can be concluded that YOLO-RFB model performs well in the task of traffic sign detection.

Fig. 6. The detection results of YOLO-RFB (left) and YOLO V4 (right) in GTSDB

5   Conclusion

This paper study the detection of traffic signs. The original YOLO V4 model is first used for experiments. It is found that the original network model has a good performance in the detection speed, but the mAP is not enough. Therefore, a traffic sign detection model YOLO-RFB based on YOLO V4 network was proposed. Based on YOLO V4 network, the main feature extraction network was pruned, and the convolution operation was replaced by RFB structure in two output feature layers. In the detection results of GTSDB, mAP of YOLO-RFB model reached 85.59%, higher than 80.83% of original YOLO V4 model. Experimental results show that the proposed model can improve the detection precision obviously while the detection rate remains stable.

While this article on the traffic sign detection task had certain research results, but there are still some problems deserves further research, the model still has a lot of optimization and improvement in future work, the model will be looking for more suitable for traffic sign detection feature extraction of the network and data sets, further enhance the speed of the model test and precision.

References

1. Zhang, X.Y., Gao, H.B., Zhao, J.H., Zhou, M.: Overview of autonomous driving technology based on deep learning. J. Tsinghua Univ. (Nat. Sci. Ed.) **58**(04), 438–444 (2018)
2. Han, S., Kang, J., Min, K., Choi, J.: DiLO: direct light detection and ranging odometry based on spherical range images for autonomous driving. ETRI J. **43**(4), 603–616 (2021)
3. Bochkovskiy, A., Wang, C.Y., Liao, H.Y.M.: YOLO V4: optimal speed and accuracy of object detection. arXiv preprint arXiv:2004.10934 (2020)
4. Wang, C.Y., Liao, H.Y.M., Wu, Y.H., et al.: CSPNet: a new backbone that can enhance learning capability of CNN. In: Proceedings of the IEEE/CVF Conference on Computer Vision and Pattern Recognition Workshops, pp. 390–391 (2020)
5. He, K., Zhang, X., Ren, S., et al.: Spatial pyramid pooling in deep convolutional networks for visual recognition. IEEE Trans. Pattern Anal. Mach. Intell. **37**(9), 1904–1916 (2015)
6. Mei, Y., Fan, Y., Zhang, Y., et al.: Pyramid attention networks for image restoration. arXiv preprint arXiv:2004.13824 (2020)
7. Yun, S., Han, D., Oh, S.J., et al.: CutMix: regularization strategy to train strong classifiers with localizable features. In: Proceedings of the IEEE/CVF International Conference on Computer Vision, pp. 6023–6032 (2019)
8. Liu, S., Huang, D.: Receptive field block net for accurate and fast object detection. In: Proceedings of the European Conference on Computer Vision (ECCV), pp. 385–400 (2018)
9. Stallkamp, J., Schlipsing, M., Salmen, J., et al.: The German traffic sign recognition benchmark: a multi-class classification competition. In: The 2011 International Joint Conference on Neural Networks, pp. 1453–1460. IEEE (2011)
10. Houben, S., Stallkamp, J., Salmen, J., et al.: Detection of traffic signs in real-world images: the German traffic sign detection benchmark. In: The 2013 International Joint Conference on Neural Networks (IJCNN), pp. 1–8. IEEE (2013)
11. Stallkamp, J., Schlipsing, M., Salmen, J., Igel, C.: Man vs. computer: benchmarking machine learning algorithms for traffic sign recognition. Neural Netw. **32**, 323–332 (2012). https://doi.org/10.1016/j.neunet.2012.02.016
12. Yu, J., Jiang, Y., Wang, Z., et al.: UnitBox: an advanced object detection network. In: Proceedings of the 24th ACM International Conference on Multimedia, pp. 516–520 (2016)
13. Zheng, Z., Wang, P., Liu, W., et al.: Distance-IoU loss: faster and better learning for bounding box regression. In: Proceedings of the AAAI Conference on Artificial Intelligence, vol. 34, no. 07, pp. 12993–13000 (2020)

14. Redmon, J., Farhadi, A.: YOLOV3: an incremental improvement. arXiv preprint arXiv:1804. 02767 (2018)
15. Liu, W., Anguelov, D., Erhan, D., et al.: SSD: Single Shot MultiBox Detector. Springer, Cham (2016)
16. Yao, Z., Cao, Y., Zheng, S., et al.: Cross-iteration batch normalization (2020)
17. Yin, Q., Yang, W., Ran, M., Wang, S.: FD-SSD: an improved SSD object detection algorithm based on feature fusion and dilated convolution. Signal Process. Image Commun. **98** (2021)
18. Li, F., et al.: Decoding imagined speech from EEG signals using hybrid-scale spatial-temporal dilated convolution network. J. Neural Eng. **18**(4), 0460c4 (2021). https://doi.org/10.1088/1741-2552/ac13c0
19. Kong, D., Li, J., Zheng, J., Xu, J., Zhang, Q.: Research on fruit recognition and positioning based on you only look once version4 (YOLOv4). In: Journal of Physics: Conference Series, vol. 2005, no. 1 (2021)
20. Sharma, M., Bansal, R.K., Prakash, S., Asefi, S.: MVO algorithm based LFC design of a six-area hybrid diverse power system integrating IPFC and RFB IETE. J. Res. **67**(3), 394–407 (2021). https://doi.org/10.1080/03772063.2018.1548908

Privacy-Preserving Sharing of Mobile Sensor Data

Yin Liu[1]($\boxtimes$), Breno Dantas Cruz[2], and Eli Tilevich[3]

[1] Faculty of Information Technology, Beijing University of Technology,
Beijing 100124, China
yinliu@bjut.edu.cn
[2] Laboratory for Software Design, Iowa State University, Ames, USA
bdantasc@iastate.edu
[3] Software Innovations Lab, Virginia Tech, Blacksburg, USA
tilevich@cs.vt.edu

Abstract. To personalize modern mobile services (e.g., advertisement, navigation, healthcare) for individual users, mobile apps continuously collect and analyze sensor data. By sharing their sensor data collections, app providers can improve the quality of mobile services. However, the data privacy of both app providers and users must be protected against data leakage attacks. To address this problem, we present *differentially privatized on-device sharing of sensor data*, a framework through which app providers can safely collaborate with each other to personalize their mobile services. As a trusted intermediary, the framework aggregates the sensor data contributed by individual apps, accepting statistical queries against the combined datasets. A novel adaptive privacy-preserving scheme: 1) balances utility and privacy by computing and adding the required amount of noise to the query results; 2) incentivizes app providers to keep contributing data; 3) secures all data processing by integrating a Trusted Execution Environment. Our evaluation demonstrates the framework's efficiency, utility, and safety: all queries complete in <10 ms; the data sharing collaborations satisfy participants' dissimilar privacy/utility requirements; mobile services are effectively personalized, while preserving the data privacy of both app providers and users.

1 Introduction

Mobile services have become a crucial part of the digital economy [2], generating large and growing revenues for application providers [42]. Following the long-tail business model, app providers focus on personalizing their mobile services by constructing detailed user profiles, including inferred frequent routes, preferred activities, and daily body vitals, with services ranging between targeted advertising to healthy living tips [4]. To optimize personalization, app providers continuously collect sensor data by means of mobile apps, linked into data-sharing

Y. Liu and B. D. Cruz—This work done in the Software Innovations Lab at Virginia Tech.

S. Deng et al. (Eds.): MobiCASE 2021, LNICST 434, pp. 19–41, 2022.
https://doi.org/10.1007/978-3-030-99203-3_2

networks within the same device or across other media (e.g., clouds), thereby creating larger collections for constructing user profiles [8]. For example, numerous location-based apps (e.g., Google Map, Uber, and Yelp) collect geolocations when each respective app is in operation. If the user frequents the same geolocations when using different mobile apps, these locations are "favorite," a piece of information that can be used to personalize location-based services.

However, due to data privacy concerns, app providers often hesitate to share sensor data: their collaborators may accidentally expose or even intentionally disclose the shared data, damaging reputation and the bottom line [34,36]. Since it is the end user who owns all device data, the app provider's privacy directly impacts user privacy. That is, leaking the shared data threatens the privacy of app providers and users. Hence, there is great need and potential benefit in providing holistic mechanisms for sharing mobile sensor data that preserve the privacy of both app providers and users.

To share the sensor data collected by their mobile apps, app providers can use cloud-based services. Each app uploads its collected data to the cloud, which aggregates and analyzes the results. The data privacy concerns of cloud-based processing of sensor data include: (a) cyber attackers can steal uploaded data by exploiting cloud server's vulnerabilities [1]; (b) insiders or careless employees can expose private data to the public [45]; (c) governments can legally force IT companies to reveal their cloud-stored data [43]. In fact, a growing number of privacy tips recommend disabling cloud-based storage and processing altogether with restrictive network access permissions [16] and network blocking apps [17]. Finally, network connectivity/congestion issues can render cloud-based processing infeasible.

Mobile apps can also share their sensor data locally on the same device. This on-device data sharing and processing—referred to as *data onloading*—has been studied widely in the research literature [18,44,47] and adopted in industrial settings. In fact, major mobile platforms do provide standardized mechanisms for the installed apps to share data locally (i.e., "App Groups" [5] in iOS; `Intent`, `SharedPreferences`, and `ContentProvider` in Android). However, these mechanisms are designed for apps to exchange data directly. As such, they are vulnerable to privacy exploits: the receiver apps can be leaking the received data unwittingly or intentionally. An alternative is for mutually distrustful app providers to discover the commonalities of their data collections (i.e., obtain data intersections) via encryption-based Private Set Intersection (PSI) [20]. However, intersections alone are hardly ever sufficient to infer the profiles of mobile users.

In this paper, we present an on-device data-sharing framework, serving as a trusted intermediary that aggregates the sensor data contributed by the collaborating apps, which execute expressive statistical queries against the combined datasets. However, simple statistical queries can be exploited by executing exhaustive frequency queries over a complete finite set [47]. Take the body sensor data as an example: the reasonable range for systolic pressure is between 90 and 180 mm Hg. An app provider can execute queries "how many x mm Hg are there in the combined dataset." After executing 91 possible queries (i.e., different values of x in the range [90, 180]), the app provider reveals the whole dataset.

A differential privacy mechanism can alleviate the risks above (e.g., PINQ [27], GUPT [32]). However, differential privacy cannot be applied directly due to the unique challenges of our problem domain: 1) it would be impossible to assign a fixed privacy level to all collaborators, as app providers may have dissimilar privacy/utility requirements; 2) some app providers can infer user profiles from the combined datasets, contributing only minimal data; and 3) attackers can illicitly access or tamper with differential privacy operations and data. To overcome the aforementioned challenges, our approach, 1) achieves the *privacy-utility tradeoffs* that satisfy given privacy/utility requirements, 2) incentivizes app providers to keep contributing data, and 3) secures the execution of statistical queries functions by placing them in a Trusted Execution Environment (TEE), whose trusted storage persists the shared data collections.

Our target is Android[1], on which apps commonly share data with each other [41]. We realize our approach as GO-BETWEEN, a system-level service that aggregates the sensor data contributed by the collaborating apps, which can then query the service to infer user profiles. By adapting differential privacy for our problem domain, GO-BETWEEN adds adaptively customized *Laplace noise* to the query results, thus properly preserving app providers' data privacy. Specifically, GO-BETWEEN balances the utility and privacy needs of the collaborating apps. Privacy can be increased at the cost of decreasing utility and vice versa. Configured to prioritize privacy, GO-BETWEEN increases the amount of noise added to the query results, so the contributed data becomes hard to uncover. Besides, GO-BETWEEN incentivizes data contributions: the more data an app contributes, the more accurate and useful its inferred user profiles are. Moreover, GO-BETWEEN's TEE-based processing safeguards the predefined statistical queries (e.g., Count, Mean, and Std) and their data. Finally, the end-user remains in control of their data by explicitly restricting apps to share data via GO-BETWEEN and being informed of the data sharing events. The contributions of this paper are as follows:

1. An on-device framework for **differentially privatized** sharing of sensor data that is *(a)* *usable:* in dynamically adapting and balancing privacy/utility, as driven by the properties of the contributed data; *(b)* *incentivizing:* in rewarding active contributing app providers with higher utility; *(c)* *secure:* in protecting all shared data and relevant operations in TEE.
2. A general system design for privacy-preserving data sharing and processing, whose building blocks include differential privacy and TEE. The applicability of this design extends beyond our target domain.
3. A reference *implementation*—GO-BETWEEN—an Android system service, empirically *evaluated* to demonstrate its efficiency, utility, and safety: all queries execute in <10 ms; the data sharing collaborations satisfy participants' dissimilar privacy/utility requirements; mobile services are effectively personalized, while preserving the privacy for both app providers and end users.

---

[1] Android mobile platform takes ≈85% of the global mobile market [21].

2   Go-Between Overview

To motivate our approach, we present two typical application scenarios and how GO-BETWEEN addresses their requirements. Then, we overview the differential privacy theory & technologies used by GO-BETWEEN.

2.1   Typical Application Scenarios

(1) Geolocation: one of the most common types of sensor data, enables app providers to infer location-based properties of a user profile (e.g., favorite areas). To optimize personalization, app providers frequently collect and share geolocations. An empirical study has revealed that within 14 days, geolocations were shared 5,398 times across 10 different apps, which included not only mapping/navigation apps, but also social media (e.g., Facebook) and shopping apps (e.g., Groupon) [3].

Consider a navigation app N that collects the user's geolocations to provide real-time traffic information. On the same device, a shopping app R records the user's geolocations independently to learn about the frequently visited areas in order to recommend shopping and dining options. Finally, an exercise app E collects the geolocations of the user's regular running routes. Since all three apps collect geolocations for different purposes, their providers may want to personalize their services, as informed by the combined dataset of their respective collections of geolocations. By querying the combined dataset (e.g., how many times the user visited a given area?), each provider can identify the user's "favorite" areas. This information can improve how each app provider tailors its services for the user, such as displaying ads specific to the favorite areas.

(2) Body vitals: another common type of sensor data, enables app providers to infer a user's health condition. Typical body vitals include temperature, pulse rate, and blood pressure. Health wearables and trackers continuously collect body vitals, sending them for processing and storage to paired devices with specialized apps. For example, a smartwatch or a blood pressure monitor would record a user's blood pressure, with the records transferred to an app running on the user's mobile phone [31,35]. A mobile app can also receive body vitals from its user's healthcare provider. For example, a recent news report points out that a healthcare record can now be downloaded to its user's mobile apps, so their providers can potentially share the downloaded records with healthcare providers and insurers [40].

Consider a blood pressure monitor app M that periodically measures and records the user's blood pressure. A smartwatch app W records the user's blood pressure at specified intervals. A personal health records app H keeps track of the user's blood pressure readings, taken during doctor's appointments. Since all these three apps collect blood pressure readings, analyzing the combined dataset of their respective collections can provide additional value to the user. For example, the frequency, the mean, and the standard deviation of all the collected readings can indicate a possible hypertension condition rather than experiencing occasional spikes of high blood pressure (due to stress).

2.2   Solution Overview

App providers[2] specify their privacy and utility requirements (e.g., high privacy and medium utility), and then share their sensor data (e.g., geolocation/blood pressure datasets) with GO-BETWEEN, which aggregates the shared data into combined datasets for app providers to query. GO-BETWEEN differentially privatizes the query results in accordance to both the properties of the shared data and the specified requirements. Through these queries, the collaborating app providers then personalize their mobile services, without revealing their raw sensor data to their collaborators.

Specifically, an app first secures a user's permission to share a certain type of sensor data. GO-BETWEEN maintains a trusted record of all apps the user has authorized to share data. A permitted app can query the combined dataset contributed by itself with a particular data type. The apps collaborate via a four-phase process: (1) apps specify their privacy and utility requirements and transfer their sensor data to GO-BETWEEN[3]; (2) upon each data deposit, GO-BETWEEN starts computing the noise scale for each built-in query operation; (3) the collaborating apps *black-box query* the combined dataset to infer the user's profile; (4) GO-BETWEEN pads the query results with a suitable amount of noise, determined by the pre-computed noise scale, and returns them.

2.3   Threat Model

Since the user owns all the collected data, the privacy of *app providers* is an integral part of *user privacy*. Nevertheless, *app providers* and *users* incur different data privacy threats, which we discuss in turn next:

App Providers. When app providers share sensor data, the process is subject to the following threats:

(a) to optimize mobile service personalization, every app provider strives to get access to as much sensor data as possible. To that end, a provider could attempt to extract their collaborators' raw data from the combined datasets. This behavior is described by a classical threat model—*honest-but-curious attack* [38]: an adversary contributes valid data but tries to learn all possible information about the combined dataset. Specifically, we assume that neither party is malicious: store fake data to render GO-BETWEEN useless. However, competing with each other, any app provider can gain a business advantage by uncovering the data in possession of its collaborators. For example, through legitimate frequency queries for each discrete data item, an app can discover the data collections possessed by the other apps.

---

[2] An app provider can have multiple apps, while an app has one provider only. For ease of exposition, we assume a one-to-one correspondence between a provider and an app, so we can use the terms "app provider" and "app" interchangeably.

[3] Each data type has its own combined dataset.

(b) to prevent the above attack, some app providers may limit their data contribution as much as possible, while taking advantage of their collaborators by inferring user profiles from the combined datasets.

(c) to illicitly obtain the collected sensor data, malicious parties may perpetrate attacks to access the combined datasets.

Mobile Users. Irrespective of how app providers share sensor data, mobile users deeply care about (a) which part of their data will be shared and (b) which app providers are involved in the sharing process.

Behavioral Model. As mentioned above, we assume that the app providers act as *honest-but-curious parties* that would not maliciously contribute fake data. To personalize mobile services in the absence of cloud-based processing, their apps can collaborate via GO-BETWEEN to improve the quality of their services and deliver a mutually beneficial outcome. Hence, rationally behaving apps would avoid any actions that would distort the subsequent statistical queries and cause all parties involved to lose out as a result. Further, by making use of machine learning or deep learning algorithms to identify outliers that deviate from the general data distribution, modern anomaly detection (i.e., outlier detection) can identify and exclude those apps that maliciously contribute fake data [19,37]. In addition, we envision app providers forming a contractual obligation for using GO-BETWEEN that regulates resource contribution, profit distribution, and commercial credibility, explicitly proscribing the intentional depositing of fake sensor data. These mechanisms create a disincentive for apps to maliciously deposit fake data.

Countermeasures. To ensure the data privacy of app providers, our approach introduces the following countermeasures:

(a) to defend against *honest-but-curious attacks*, all query results are differentially privatized, so the participating app providers cannot recreate the combined datasets (Sect. 3.1 Sect. 3.2).

(b) to discourage limited data sharing, a query result's accuracy is positively correlated with the size of the querier's data contribution, thus incentivizing large-scale sharing (Sect. 3.3)

(c) to prevent the combined datasets from being illicitly accessed, all shared data and relevant operations take place in a Trusted Execution Environment (TEE) (Sect. 4.1).

(d) to keep the user in control, all sharing-related information (the list of apps, the data type, and query, etc.) can be routed to the user for examination and approval. The user can opt out from receiving this information.

2.4   Enabling Theory and Technologies

(1) Differential Privacy (DP) protects an individual's private information[4] from unauthorized discovery [10]. More formally, a *database D* is a database of

---

[4] Hereafter, *individual* refers to *an app provider*, and *private information* refers to the sensor data collected by a provider.

records in a *data universe* U. Each record contains an individual's private data. Differential Privacy defines two databases D and D' as *neighboring databases* if they differ by exactly one record. A *mechanism* M is a randomized function that maps D to output R.

Definition 1: ε-differentially private mechanism. Given $\varepsilon \geq 0$, M is ε-differentially private, iff for all neighboring databases (D, D'), and for any sets of outputs $S \subseteq R$:

$$Pr[M(D) \in S] \leq e^{\varepsilon} Pr[M(D') \in S] \tag{1}$$

Definition 2: sequential composition. Given a set of *mechanisms* $M = M_1, ..., M_n$, sequentially executed on a database, with each M_i providing ε_i-differential privacy guarantee, the total guarantee provided by M is:

$$\sum_{i=1}^{n} \varepsilon_i \tag{2}$$

Definition 3: global sensitivity. For a query $f : D \to R$; D,D' are *neighboring databases*, the global sensitivity of f is:

$$\Delta f = Max_{D,D'} |f(D) - f(D')| \tag{3}$$

The value of Δf (i.e., global sensitivity of f) indicates the maximal difference between the query results on D and D'.

Definition 4: upper bound of ε [24]. Given a database D' with $n-1$ records sampled from D (i.e., $D' \subset D$ and $|D'| = |D| - 1$), the probability of discovering the record in the database D (i.e., ρ), the number of records (n), the global sensitivity of query f (i.e., Δf), and the maximal difference between query results of each possible combination of D' (i.e., Δv):

$$\varepsilon \leq \frac{\Delta f}{\Delta v} ln \frac{(n-1)\rho}{1-\rho} \tag{4}$$

(2) Laplace Mechanism [11] adds independent noise to the actual query results. $Lap(\mu, b)$ represents the noise sampled from a *Laplace Distribution* with the scale factor of b and location factor of μ. The *Laplace distribution* is a double exponential distribution, in which the scale factor b is positively correlated with the amplitude, thus determining the confidence level in the noisy results. Briefly, b determines the amount of *Laplace noise* to add. Usually, we omit μ and use $Lap(b)$ as the added noise.

Definition 5 — noise scale. To satisfy ε-differential privacy for query f, use scaled symmetric noise $Lap(b)$ with $b = \Delta f/\varepsilon$, that is:

$$Lap(\Delta f/\varepsilon) \tag{5}$$

By setting the location factor of μ with the actual result of query $f(D)$, we can get the privatized value: $f(D) + Lap(\Delta f/\varepsilon)$ that ensures the ε-differential privacy.

Definition 6 — noise scale for a query sequence. To satisfy ε-differential privacy for a query sequence $f_1, ..., f_n$, use scaled symmetric noise:

$$Lap(\sum_i \Delta f_i / \varepsilon) \tag{6}$$

(3) Trusted Execution Environment (TEE) [13] provides hardware support for handling sensitive data. TEE (1) partitions the CPU into the normal world for common applications and the secure world for trusted applications; the secure world prevents external entities without authorization from accessing trusted applications; (2) provides trusted storage to persist sensitive data, which can only be accessed via the provided API; (3) provides a secure communication channel for external peripherals. *Open-TEE* [26] virtualizes TEE via a software framework. By conforming to the GlobalPlatform Specifications of TEE, Open-TEE hosts trusted applications, in lieu of a hardware-based TEE. Known as an efficient "virtual TEE," Open-TEE features small storage and memory footprints as well as short start and restart latencies for the trusted applications.

3   Applying and Complementing DP

We first explain by example how we apply differential privacy (DP) to defend against the aforementioned honest-but-curious attacks. Then we discuss how we complemented DP to meet the privacy requirements in our target domain.

3.1   From Theory to Practice

(1) Honest-but-curious attacks: We further develop the scenario in Sect. 2.1 that shares body vitals. Consider the worst-case scenario: only two apps—H and M—share their collected blood pressure readings.

As shown in Fig. 1, H stores its blood pressure readings into the combined dataset (i.e., D—the table on the left). Then, H queries for the frequency of "150", which returns "1",

D

App Provider	Systolic Pressure
H	150
H	140

D'

App Provider	Systolic Pressure
H	150
H	140
M	150

Fig. 1. The worst-case scenario of the attack.

as "150" occurs only once in the combined dataset. After that, M adds one more reading of "150" to the combined dataset (i.e., D'—the table on the right). Then, H repeats the same frequency query on the updated dataset, getting "2" as the result, meaning that "150" now appears twice. In this worst-case, H may also discover that M has stored its dataset between H's two frequency queries. Armed with this fact, H can determine it was M that stored the other value of "150."

(2) Counter-measuring with DP: Consider how DP can be applied to defend against such honest-but-curious attacks. The worst-case scenarios above can be formalized as a differential privacy problem. To put it briefly, a DP mechanism would pad each query result with noise. As an illustration, assume that H's first and second queries are padded with the noise amounts of "0.6" and "−0.5", respectively, so the final results would become "1.6" (i.e., 1 + 0.6) and "1.5" (i.e., 2 − 0.5), respectively. These fractional results about the frequency of "150" in the combined dataset still provide useful information (e.g., "1.6" and "1.5" are between 0 and 2). However, now H can no longer infer if M has contributed "150" to the dataset.

3.2 Privacy and Utility Tradeoffs

As we discussed above, differential privacy can prevent the potential breaches described in our threat model by adding the *Laplace noise* to the query results to obtain an ε-differential privacy guarantee. However, *the resulting noise scale must balance the tradeoffs between privacy and utility.* The former represents how large the noise to add, while the latter indicates how usable the noisy results are for inferring user profiles. Privacy and utility are negatively correlated: the higher is the level of privacy, the lower is utility, and vice versa.

(1) Privacy. Definition (4) determines the upper bound of ε, and Definition (5) shows the noise scale. By combining (4) (5), we obtain the lower bound of scaled noise $Lap(b)$ with:

$$b = \Delta v / ln \frac{(n-1)\rho}{1-\rho} \tag{7}$$

As per Definitions (4) and (5), ρ is the probability that the adversary can correctly guess the absence/presence of a record in the combined dataset. n is the number of records. Δv is the maximal difference between the query results of each possible combination of D'. Thus, n and Δv can be calculated based on the dataset's properties. ρ can be configured by apps in order to control the privacy level based on their specific requirements.

(2) Utility. *How accurate the query results are* and *how frequently the query is executed* determine utility:

a) For accuracy, we define the *accuracy level* (a) as the distance between the actual query result and the result with noise. We determine a via the *percent error* formula:

$$a = 100 \cdot \left| \frac{Result_{noise} - Result_{actual}}{Result_{actual}} \right| \tag{8}$$

The collaborating apps can set the required accuracy level. After adding noise, if the result of a query cannot meet the accuracy requirement set by the app, the query fails.

b) For usage frequency, we define the *usage frequency level* (u) as the invocation number of a certain query. Based on the Definition 2, for example, if an app performs a query (providing ε-differential privacy guarantee) 10 times, then the query's total differential privacy guarantee is $10 \cdot \varepsilon$. Each collaborating app can configure its usage frequency level, used to adjust the noise scale. See *Noise Increase Scheme* (Sect. 3.3-3) below for details.

3.3   Data Contribution Incentives

For app providers to be willing to keep contributing data to Go-Between, three conditions must be met:

1. The privacy level ρ should be a parameter shared across all collaborating apps. If the specified privacy level affects only the app that specifies it, the resulting perverse incentive would suggest specifying the lowest privacy level to obtain the highest utility.
2. The amount of contributed data should be commensurate with the obtained utility.
3. The more an app queries Go-Between, the more noise should be added to its privatized query results.

To meet above conditions, we introduce *global privacy level*, *bonus mechanism* and *noise increase scheme*, respectively.

(1) Global Privacy Level: For each collaborating app, we define a *contribution rate (c)*:

$$c_i = \frac{\omega_i}{\sum \omega_i}, \tag{9}$$

where ω_i is the amount of data contributed by the ith app. By weighting the *average* value of app-configured privacy levels by their contributed data's amount, Go-Between determines the *global privacy level*:

$$\rho_{global} = \sum c_i \rho_i, \tag{10}$$

where ρ_i is the *privacy level* configured by the ith app.

The *global privacy level* is used to calculate the noise scale (b) by using (7). That is, the more data an app contributes to a combined dataset, the higher the impact of the app's privacy level on the overall global privacy level. This design prevents apps with only a small contribution from specifying the lowest privacy level with the goal of accurately inferring user profiles.

(2) Bonus Mechanism: We establish a bonus mechanism that reduces the noise scale (i.e., increases the accuracy) for apps in proportion to the amount of their contributed data. To that end, Go-Between selects 10% of a given query's noise scale as the bonus: $\boldsymbol{BONUS = 10\% \cdot b_{query}}$, where b_{query} is the query's noise scale. When adjusting i^{th} app's noise scale (b_i), we use the app's *contribution rate (c)* to calculate its bonus: $c_i \cdot BONUS$, which is subtracted from the noise scale:

$$b_i = b_{query} - c_i \cdot BONUS \tag{11}$$

(3) Noise Increase Scheme: Since every query invocation accumulates ε (Definition 2), the likelihood of an attacker discovering the raw dataset is positively correlated with *usage frequency level* (u) (i.e., the number of query invocations). To reduce the risk of such discovery, GO-BETWEEN scales b_i up by u_i times (i.e., $b_i * u_i$). By increasing the noise scale proportionally to the number of query invocations, GO-BETWEEN thus maintains the ε-differential privacy.

4   System Design and Implementation

Our approach is reified by the GO-BETWEEN framework, whose design and implementation we describe in turn next.

4.1   Architecture

Figure 2 and the code snippet below show GO-BETWEEN's architecture and programming interface, respectively:

Mobile Apps configure their privacy and utility requirements, persist their individual collections of sensor data, and perform reactive queries on the combined dataset via the GO-BETWEEN API (step 1). The API interacts with GO-BETWEEN service (step 2), a system-level Android service that encodes the data (step 3) via the Encoding Protocol and executes service calls (i.e., query, persist, and configuration) via Native Interface (step 4). Finally, the data is passed to TEE to be securely operated on (step 5).

Then, TEE-based operations (i.e., Data Ops:data management, query Ops:query, and DP Ops:differential privacy operations) execute on Combined_Set, with all configurations stored securely in Configs (step 6). Finally, the results are returned from TEE to Mobile

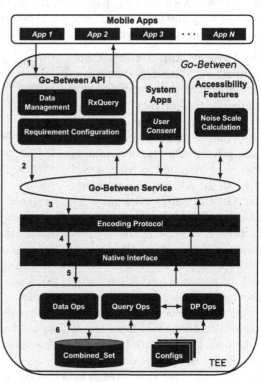

Fig. 2. System architecture.

Apps. More importantly, based on the persisted data's content and configuration, Accessibility Components calculate the noise scale for each supported query type. This feature runs on dedicated worker threads, synchronized by means of Android's `Handler` and `Message`. In addition, whenever an app issues a query request, `Go-Between Service` can be configured to notify the permission granting app (i.e., `User Consent`), so the end-user can approve/decline the request to proceed.

Go-Between is integrated into the Android Platform as part of its standard SDK: `Go-Between API` and `Accessibility Components` into the Android Framework Layer, `Go-Between Service` into both the Framework and Native Library Layers, `Encoding Protocol` into the Native Library Layer, and `Native Interface` into the Hardware Abstraction Layer. Since inadvertent misconfigurations or system attacks can cause data leakage, `Combined_Set` and `Configs` are placed in TEE to become hard-to-compromise, while `Data Ops`, `Query Ops`, and `DP Ops` run in TEE as trusted operations.

4.2   Privacy Mechanism

Go-Between's adaptively parameterized privacy mechanism: 1) configures each app's privacy and utility requirements, 2) determines the required noise scale and pads the query results with the suitable amount of noise.

(1) Privacy and Utility Configuration. With Go-Between, developers of mobile apps can configure the privacy and utility levels for each query. However, unless those developers are data privacy experts, determining the exact required privacy levels is hard. To address this problem, the Go-Between API provides human-readable levels, as shown in Table 1, to express the requirements, which include the *privacy level* (i.e., privacy requirement) and the *accuracy level & usage frequency level* (i.e., utility requirement). Each of them is divided into five consecutive levels from lowest to highest. Queries with higher *privacy levels* need more noise added

Table 1. Privacy & utility requirements

Privacy$^\alpha$		Accuracy$^\beta$		Usage Freq.$^\gamma$	
Level	Pr.	Level	Err.	Level	Times
Lowest	70%	Lowest	50%	Lowest	1
Public	50%	Estimate	30%	Rare	5
Default	20%	Default	20%	Default	10
Critical	5%	Exact	10%	Frequent	50
Highest	1%	Highest	5%	Highest	100

$^\alpha$*Privacy level* is the probability of an adversary correctly discovering the combined dataset's raw data, used to calculate the noise scale.
$^\beta$*Accuracy level* is the *% error* as per formula (8), a noisy result's utility for inferring user profiles.
$^\gamma$*Usage frequency level*, a query's invocation #, used to calculate a query's noise scale, especially in a sequence of queries.

to the result, and vice versa. The lower the *accuracy level*, the more the noisy and the original results differ, and the less useful the noisy results are for inferring user profiles. With the restriction on the *usage frequency level*, ε-differential privacy can be ensured even if the apps continuously invoke a certain query or perform a fused sequence of queries.

Consider applying the predefined query Mean, which obtains the *mean* value of the combined dataset, to our running example of sharing blood pressure readings. Suppose the personal health records app H prefers higher privacy and utility levels of Mean, so it may set the privacy level to Critical, the accuracy level to Exact, and the usage frequency level to Frequent; the smartwatch app W prioritizes privacy only, so it could configure the requirements as Highest, Estimate, and Rare, respectively; the blood pressure monitor app M, with regular privacy and utility requirements, may set all parameters to Default. Based on a given configuration, GO-BETWEEN automatically calculates the required noise scale, and determines how to execute each query.

(2) Noise Scale Calculation. Once apps specify their privacy/utility requirements and persist their datasets into TEE, GO-BETWEEN calculates the noise scale for each query in two steps: 1) determine the *global privacy level* (i.e., ρ_{global}) for the combined dataset contributed by the collaborating apps, 2) use ρ_{global} to determine the noise scale (i.e., b) required to fulfill the privacy/utility requirements of each app. In addition, GO-BETWEEN incentivizes the collaborating apps to keep contributing data (as discussed in Sect. 3.3).

To illustrate how GO-BETWEEN determines the global privacy level, consider the running example of apps H, W, and M setting their respective privacy levels for the Mean query to Critical (i.e., ρ_H), Highest (i.e., ρ_W), and Default (i.e., ρ_M), respectively. GO-BETWEEN first looks up the actual probability values for these human-readable levels as per Table 1: $\rho_H = 5\%$, $\rho_W = 1\%$, $\rho_M = 20\%$. Then, by weighting the average value of these probabilities by the data collection size of each app, GO-BETWEEN determines the global privacy level (as per *formula* 10): $\rho_{global} = c_H\rho_H + c_W\rho_W + c_M\rho_M$, where c is the data *contribution rate* of each app. Because GO-BETWEEN updates ρ_{global} whenever new apps join an existing data sharing collaboration, ρ_{global} always reflects the actual privacy requirement of the collaborating apps.

Having determined the global privacy level (ρ_{global}), GO-BETWEEN plugs the resulting value into the *formula* 7 (Sect. 3.2) that calculates the noise scale of each predefined query: $b = \Delta v / ln\frac{(n-1)\rho}{1-\rho}$, with ρ becoming ρ_{global}, and n becoming the *size of the combined dataset*. To determine Δv, $n - 1$ records are sampled from the combined dataset by performing each query on n different data combinations (i.e., $\binom{n}{n-1}$). For example, for a combined dataset of 1000 items, select 999 (i.e., 1000 - 1) records, and perform a given query on them obtaining a result. Then, repeat this process to obtain the query results of 1000 different data combinations. Next, use the max and min results to calculate the Δv for this query. Finally, calculate this query's noise scale using the *formula* 7 above. GO-BETWEEN obtains the noise scale for each predefined query, persisting the results into TEE.

To determine the final noise scale for each app, GO-BETWEEN executes the *bonus mechanism* and applies the *noise increase scheme*. In our running example, suppose the *contribution rates* (c) of apps H, W, and M are c_H, c_W, and c_M, respectively, while their *usage frequency levels* (u) for the Mean query are Frequent (i.e., u_H), Rare (i.e., u_W), and Default (i.e., u_M), respectively. These levels correspond to the max # of invocations: $u_H = 50, u_W = 5, u_M = 10$ (as per Table 1). Then the actual noise scale of Mean for each app is calculated using: $b_i = u_i \cdot (b_{query} - c_i \cdot BONUS)$, where $b_{query} = \Delta v / ln \frac{(n-1)\rho_{global}}{1-\rho_{global}}$, with $\{u_i | u_H, u_W, u_M\}$ and $\{c_i | c_H, c_W, c_M\}$ (as per *formula* 11). For example, each time app H performs Mean on the combined dataset, GO-BETWEEN ensures ε-differential privacy by adding the *Laplace noise* to the query result with the noise scale: $b_H = u_H \cdot (b_{mean} - c_H \cdot BONUS)$.

5   Evaluation

The following questions drive our evaluation. **Q1. Feasibility**: Does GO-BETWEEN offer acceptable performance levels? **Q2. Utility**: Do GO-BETWEEN's data sharing collaborations satisfy dissimilar app requirements? **Q3. Safety**: How effectively does GO-BETWEEN eliminate the threats of apps uncovering their competitors' raw data?

5.1   Experimental Setup

(1) Experimental Environment Choice. We implement and evaluate GO-BETWEEN using the official Android source code release, Android Open Source Project (AOSP), which provides an official virtualized execution environment[5] for testing and debugging Android apps. Because its standard distribution excludes a TEE component, we integrated Open-TEE[6] with AOSP by adding the Open-TEE source code to the main codebase of AOSP and building them together into a single executable image. To maximize the number of Android apps compatible with GO-BETWEEN, while having access to as many of advanced Android features as possible, we use the Android Lollipop 5.1 release, currently run by 14.4% Android devices (the third highest percentage among the 13 most popular Android platform versions [15]) and has cumulatively covered 80.2% devices (cumulative distribution [14]).

(2) Software and Hardware. The main system components of our experiments are: platform version is Lollipop; host OS is Linux; CPU (MHz) is 3599.943; cache size (KB) is 2048; and TEE solution is Open-TEE. Without loss of generality, we assume a standard setup: device sensors are enabled, and the involved apps are granted permissions to collect sensor data.

(3) Benchmarks. To establish a performance baseline, we create a set of benchmarks that isolate the GO-BETWEEN's operations that store data collections and perform the pre-defined queries. In addition, the software-based virtualization of TEE is bound to exhibit performance levels inferior to those offered by hardware-based implementations. Hence, our performance results not in any way unfairly

---

[5] A common practice for studying various performance trade-offs on the Android platform [6].

[6] A portable framework for code to run on any standardized TEEs.

benefit our approach. Since w.r.t. performance, our evaluation goals are only to demonstrate that it is feasible to offer a GO-BETWEEN-like service locally on the device, in the presence of an actual hardware-based TEE, the overhead of using GO-BETWEEN can only decrease.

5.2   Evaluation Design

Q1. Feasibility: Despite the computationally intensive nature of data processing, GO-BETWEEN must operate unintrusively, with performance overheads comparable to those of similar Android system services. In light of these evaluation objectives, we design a set of representative micro-benchmarks and application scenarios and measure the performance of the GO-BETWEEN-related functionality. Then we compare these results with Android App's standard response time limitation (i.e., Application Not Responding (ANR) error). Specifically, we measure the total execution time (T_{total}) it takes to execute a GO-BETWEEN operation with realistic data by a single app to understand service's performance impact. Specifically, we measure the total execution time taken by storeData, Mean, Std, CountOne, and CountFreq GO-BETWEEN operations. GO-BETWEEN calculates noise scales concurrently on separate worker threads, whose performance we chose not to evaluate as they leave the main execution unperturbed.

Q2. Utility: We follow our *running example-I* (Sect. 2.1): with apps N (App1), E (App2), and R (App3) collecting geolocation data and collaborating via GO-BETWEEN to discover their user's favorite locations. The user in this experiment is the Yeti[7], who according to Nepali folklore haunts the Himalayas [23]. As it turns out, the Yeti is a sophisticated and demanding mobile user. Due to the need to keep his existence inconspicuous, the Yeti refuses to upload any of the sensor output of his apps to the cloud; besides, the network infrastructure of Himalaya renders any cloud services inaccessible. Nevertheless, Yeti demands highly personalized services that customize the actively used apps to his profile.

App1, App2, and App3 deposit with GO-BETWEEN 100, 50, and 20 Himalayan geolocations, respectively. The experiment queries the combined dataset to determine the Yeti's favorite locations (i.e., CountFreq). The input is a square area, while the output is the number of times the Yeti visited the area. Each of the apps queries three areas, with different privacy and utility requirements. We seek answers to these questions: 1) how beneficial is GO-BETWEEN in discovering the Yeti's favorite locations as compared to using only the data of individual apps? and 2) how do the privacy and utility requirements affect the GO-BETWEEN's results?

Q3. Safety: We follow our *running example-II* (Sect. 2.1): a healthcare app H collects snapshots of systolic blood pressure (SYS). H applies GO-BETWEEN to persist its data collection of 100 records into TEE for collaborating with other apps, and sets its privacy and utility requirements as Highest (i.e., privacy level

---

[7] The Yeti is a metaphor that describes any real-world user with a similar behavioral profile in this application scenario.

ρ_H), `Default` (i.e., accuracy level a_H), `Default` (i.e., usage frequency level u_H). Then, we simulate the attack scenario—*Revealing raw data:*

Because the reasonable range for SYS is between 90 and 180 mm Hg, H's competitor app C performs `CountOne`[8] on all possible values to discover the combined dataset's raw data. Further, to maximize the opportunity to uncover the raw data of H, the app C sets its requirement as `Lowest` (i.e., privacy level ρ_H), `Highest` (i.e., accuracy level a_H), `Default` (i.e., usage frequency level u_H). Hence, it can contribute a large number of records to heighten the weights, thus decreasing the privacy level of the entire dataset. Then, app C performs `CountOne` on the combined dataset to obtain the frequency of each possible SYS occurrence. Finally, it compares these query results with its own dataset to infer app H's raw data. We evaluate with app C's data sizes of 20^9, 100, 1000, 5000 to a) verify whether our approach can preserve the data privacy for each collaborating app; b) to determine the resiliency of our privacy protection as a relation to the size of the attacker's contributed dataset.

5.3 Results

Q1. Feasibility: As discussed in Sect. 5.2, we benchmark the respective latencies of persisting data (i.e., `storeData`), and querying the combined datasets (i.e., `Mean`, `Std`, `CountOne`, and `CountFreq`) with dissimilar data sizes (i.e., 20, 100, 1000, 5000). As shown in Fig. 3, neither of the predefined queries exceeds 10 ms in latency, due to their low asymptotic complexity O(n). For `storeData`, as the data size grows, so does the execution time (12 to 48 ms), as the increases in data size are directly proportional to the work performed by the data encoding/decoding and storing processes. To sum up, the GO-BETWEEN API operations execute within the maximal threshold imposed by the Android platform (response time < 5 s) and expected by end-users (response < 1 s [29]); even the longest observed response time taken by `store-Data` ($\approx$48 ms) is still within these boundaries.

Q2. Utility: As shown in Fig. 4 (in square), without GO-BETWEEN, the query of "how many times the Yeti visited a given area", performed by App1, App2, and App3 returns 17, 45, and 0, respectively, for *Area-A*; 31, 1, and 6 for *Area-B*; and 10, 0, and 8 for *Area-C*. Hence, App1 would think *Area-B* as Yeti's favorite, App2 *Area-A*, and App3 *Area-C*. However, in fact, the Yeti's favorite area is A (62 visits overall), so without GO-BETWEEN the Yeti would be left very unhappy with the customizations of App1 and App3.

We study the utility of GO-BETWEEN under different requirements. Figure 4 shows (in bubble shape), with the "Default" settings for all requirements, the subject apps obtain 63.15, 66.96, and 58.89 visits of *Area-A* (i.e., the bubble in the upper left corner). The ε-differential privacy of these results is based on the configured "Default" privacy level for each app. The noise added to these results

---

[8] `CountOne(m)` queries "how many times does value 'm' appear in the combined dataset?".

[9] As a rule of thumb of practical statistical analysis, the minimum sample size is typically between 20 and 30 [30].

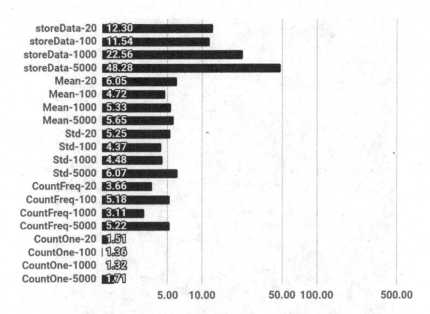

Fig. 3. Performance (log scale with millisecond).

is based on each app's noise scale (n) of this query. Because App1 contributes more data than App2, which contributes more data than App3, $n_1 < n_2 < n_3$. GO-BETWEEN adds the least noise to App1's result, making it most accurate (i.e., 63.15 is the closest to the actual result of 62). Although it cannot be guaranteed that App1's results would always be the closest to the actual value, the smallest noise scale maximizes such chances, in conformance with *Laplace distribution*.

Setting the privacy level to "Highest" reduces accuracy the most. As shown in the bubble in the middle left of Fig. 4, with the highest level, the query results for *Area-A* become: 74.81 (App1), 45.50 (App2), and 77.98 (App3), deviating greatly from the actual result of 62. Hence, one can increase privacy at the cost of accuracy, and each app can specify the accuracy level as required for a given scenario. To maximize accuracy, apps set their privacy level to "Lowest" and query for *Area-B* (actual value: 38). Indeed, the results' accuracy increases: 39.78 (App1), 39.07 (App2), 35.53 (App3) (i.e., the bubble in the middle). Notice that the result for App2 (i.e., 39.07) is closer to the actual value than that of App1 (i.e., 39.78). For very small noise scales, the amount of added noise is small as well, making the results of App1 and App2 close to each other. Despite the differences in the added noise, the results still conform to the *Laplace distribution*.

As discussed in Sect. 4.2, the app contributing more data increases its power to impact the combined dataset's privacy level. To evaluate this feature, we let App1 and App2 (respectively contributing 100 and 50 geolocations) set their privacy levels to "Highest", while keeping it "Lowest" for App3 (contributing only 20 geolocations). The results (i.e., the bubble in the bottom middle of Fig. 4—App1: 46.05; App2: 27.97; App3: 31.69) show that even with "Lowest"

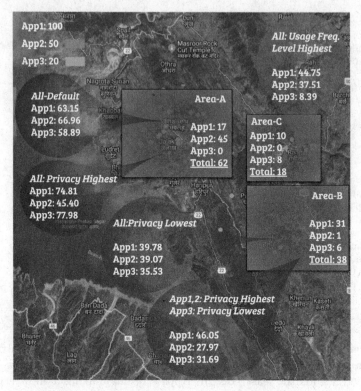

(a) the **square** (i.e., Area-A, B, and C) contains the number of the Yeti's visits to the area, as reflected in each app's individual data collection (i.e., without GO-BETWEEN and the combined dataset). E.g., square"Area-A" shows that App1 records 17 visits of the Yeti to this area, App2 45 visits, and App3 0 visits. So, the actual number of the Yeti's visits to the Area-A is 62 (i.e., 17 + 45 + 0).

(b) the **bubble shape** contains the query results for each app using GO-BETWEEN with the combined dataset. E.g., the bubble in the upper left corner shows that with the "Default" settings for all requirements ("All-Default"), the subject apps obtain 63.15 ("App1"), 66.96 ("App2"), and 58.89 ("App3") visits to "Area-A".

Fig. 4. Utility of GO-BETWEEN.

privacy level for App3, the global privacy level increases, as the other apps contribute more data.

As discussed in Sect. 4.2, the usage frequency level also trades privacy for accuracy: the more a query executes, the easier it is for an adversary to discover the raw data of others. GO-BETWEEN mitigates this risk by increasing the noise scale in accordance with the observed usage frequency, which corresponds to the max number a query has been invoked. To evaluate it, we let all apps set their usage frequency to "Highest", meaning that the query can be repeated up to a 100 times. The results (the bubble in the upper right corner) become 44.75 (App1), 37.51 (App2), and 8.39 (App3), while the actual value is 18. That is, by setting the usage frequency level to "Highest", apps can perform continuous frequent invocations of queries whose results would not be as accurate.

Q3. Safety: Defending against the attack of revealing raw data: App H deposits with GO-BETWEEN a dataset containing 20 duplicate systolic blood pressure (SYS) snapshots of 150 mm Hg. App C perpetrates an attack to discover H's raw data, by setting its privacy level to "Lowest" and performing the query `CountOne(150)` (i.e., "how many times does value 150 appear in the combined dataset?"). Table 2 shows that, with the size of its con-

Table 2. Safety of GO-BETWEEN*

Size	Contribution rate	Noise scale	Actual value	Noisy value
20	16.7%	3.23	20	11.26
100	50.0%	2.02	20	22.14
1000	90.9%	1.31	20	20.39
5000	98.0%	1.07	20	19.49

*As a control group, we also reproduced a classic *honest-but-curious* attack: *Without* GO-BETWEEN, the attacker always uncovers the actual readings.

tributed dataset growing (the "Size" column), C's contribution rate increases (the "Contribution Rate" column), noise scale decreases (the "Noise Scale" column), and query results (the "Noisy Value" column) approach the actual value (i.e., 20).

With C's "Lowest" privacy level, as the size of C's contributed dataset increases, the global privacy level decreases, producing a fairly small noise scale to privatize the query results. Therefore, with little added noise, the C's query results are close to the actual values. Note that the added noise conforms to the *Laplace distribution*, whose peak's sharpness is controlled by the noise scale. The smaller the noise scale, the sharper the *Laplace distribution*'s peak, so the added noise fluctuates less, increasing the confidence in the accuracy of the query results. That is, with the actual value of 20, querying a dataset of 1000 items produces 20.39, while querying a dataset of 5000 items produces 19.49. Although 20.39 is closer to 20 than 19.49 is, the second query's noise scale is lower, increasing the attacker's confidence in its ability to discover the actual value. However, GO-BETWEEN still prevents the attacker from determining what the exact raw data is.

To summarize, a) with high contribution rates, attackers may roughly guess what the raw data is, while being unable to discover the exact values; b) to reduce the risk of such attacks discovering the raw data, collaborating apps can increase the global privacy level by contributing more data.

6   Discussion

(1) Data privacy of the app provider and the mobile user: Since all shared data belongs to the device user, improving the data privacy of app providers also improves user privacy. In contrast to those privacy preservation approaches that focus exclusively on user privacy without any regard for the business aspirations of app providers, we strive to take a more holistic approach. We acknowledge that app providers need to achieve their business objectives of personalizing mobile services and provide them with a convenient privacy-preserving framework to accomplish that. In essence, our goal is to take away a major motivation for app providers to illicitly bypass the privacy protection mechanisms in place. Our framework enables app providers to accomplish their business objectives in a privacy-preserving fashion, thus implicitly improving end user privacy.

(2) Applicability: *(a) For other platforms:* although our reference implementation is Android-based, our approach's complemented differential privacy (Sect. 3) and system design (Sect. 4) are applicable to any Android release or other mobile platforms. *(b) For other scenarios:* our approach can benefit other data sharing scenarios. For example, sharing data at the edge, (e.g., smart home, autonomous driving), often involves mutually distrustful parties that can apply our approach to personalize their services by sharing data without compromising their data privacy. *(c) For other queries:* our functional and reactive query interfaces can be extended for additional queries, thus further increasing our approach's applicability.

7   Related Work

Data Privacy. Differential privacy [10] prevents attackers from discovering private information. Based on this concept, Airavat [39] provides differential privacy guarantees for cloud-based MapReduce computations. The PINQ [27] and GUPT [32] libraries add a unified amount of noise to raw data for privacy-preserving data analysis. Vu et al. [46] automatically detect the user's privacy requirements by determining the noise scale with a neural network model. Miller et al. [28] provide security protocols for clients to securely communicate with a non-trusted server. Gaboardi et al. [12] enable users, unaware of differential privacy mechanics, to generate privacy-preserving datasets that support statistical queries. GO-BETWEEN differs by inferring user profiles on-device, with its ε-differential privacy augmented with *privacy & utility tradeoffs* and *data contribution incentives.*

Collaboration Among Distrustful Parties. By using encryption techniques, Private Set Intersection (PSI) enables two parties to find the intersection of their private datasets, without revealing any data outside the intersection. Kiss et al. [22] applies PSI techniques to find the set intersection of differently sized datasets in mobile applications, but not on-device as in our approach. PSI protocols have been also implemented for smartphones. For example, CrowdShare [7] shares Internet connectivity and other resources across Android devices. Secure Function Evaluation (SFE) techniques allow mutually distrustful parties to evaluate the properties of private sets without revealing them. Previous work on SFE defines the adversarial models, decreases communication complexity, and improves efficiency/security definitions [9,25,33]. In contrast, to share data, GO-BETWEEN relies neither on encryption nor on the SFE techniques. Distrustful parties can effectively collaborate via GO-BETWEEN that balances their privacy & utility requirements by automatically determining the required noise scale.

8 Conclusion

We have presented on-device sharing of sensor data to personalize mobile services while protecting data privacy. Powered by an adaptive privacy mechanism, our approach: (1) satisfies the dissimilar privacy and utility requirements of the collaborating apps, (2) incentivizes the apps to keep contributing data, and (3) protects sensitive data and operations in a trusted execution environment. The evaluation demonstrates our approach's feasibility, utility, and safety.

Acknowledgements. The authors thank the anonymous reviewers, whose insightful comments helped improve this paper. NSF supported this research through the grant #1717065.

References

1. CVE-2016-6540 (2016). https://cve.mitre.org/cgi-bin/cvename.cgi?name=CVE-2016-6540
2. Acquisti, A., Taylor, C., Wagman, L.: The economics of privacy. J. Econ. Lit. **54**(2), 442–92 (2016)
3. Almuhimedi, H., et al.: Your location has been shared 5,398 times! a field study on mobile app privacy nudging. In: Proceedings of the 33rd Annual ACM Conference on Human Factors in Computing Systems, pp. 787–796 (2015)
4. Anderson, C., Andersson, M.P.: Long tail (2004)
5. Apple Inc.: App groups entitlement (2017). https://developer.apple.com/documentation/bundleresources/entitlements/com_apple_security_application-groups
6. Armando, A., Merlo, A., Migliardi, M., Verderame, L.: Would you mind forking this process? A denial of service attack on android (and some countermeasures). In: Gritzalis, D., Furnell, S., Theoharidou, M. (eds.) SEC 2012. IAICT, vol. 376, pp. 13–24. Springer, Heidelberg (2012). https://doi.org/10.1007/978-3-642-30436-1_2
7. Asokan, N., et al.: CrowdShare: secure mobile resource sharing. In: Jacobson, M., Locasto, M., Mohassel, P., Safavi-Naini, R. (eds.) ACNS 2013. LNCS, vol. 7954, pp. 432–440. Springer, Heidelberg (2013). https://doi.org/10.1007/978-3-642-38980-1_27
8. Binns, R., Lyngs, U., Van Kleek, M., Zhao, J., Libert, T., Shadbolt, N.: Third party tracking in the mobile ecosystem. In: Proceedings of the 10th ACM Conference on Web Science, pp. 23–31 (2018)
9. Canetti, R.: Security and composition of multiparty cryptographic protocols. J. Cryptol. **13**(1), 143–202 (2000)
10. Dwork, C.: Differential privacy: a survey of results. In: Agrawal, M., Du, D., Duan, Z., Li, A. (eds.) TAMC 2008. LNCS, vol. 4978, pp. 1–19. Springer, Heidelberg (2008). https://doi.org/10.1007/978-3-540-79228-4_1
11. Dwork, C., McSherry, F., Nissim, K., Smith, A.: Calibrating noise to sensitivity in private data analysis. In: Halevi, S., Rabin, T. (eds.) TCC 2006. LNCS, vol. 3876, pp. 265–284. Springer, Heidelberg (2006). https://doi.org/10.1007/11681878_14
12. Gaboardi, M., Honaker, J., King, G., Nissim, K., Ullman, J., Vadhan, S.: PSI: a private data sharing interface. arXiv:1609.04340 (2016)

13. GlobalPlatform: GlobalPlatform, TEE system architecture, technical report (2011). www.globalplatform.org/specificationsdevice.asp
14. Google: Android studio - select the minimum API level (2018). https://developer.android.com/studio/projects/create-project
15. Google: Distribution dashboard (2018). https://developer.android.com/about/dashboards
16. Google: Connect to the network (2019). https://developer.android.com/training/basics/network-ops/connecting
17. Google Play Store: Noroot firewall (2019). https://play.google.com/store/apps/details?id=app.greyshirts.firewall&hl=en
18. Han, S., Philipose, M.: The case for onloading continuous high-datarate perception to the phone. In: Presented as Part of the 14th Workshop on Hot Topics in Operating Systems (2013)
19. Hendrycks, D., Mazeika, M., Dietterich, T.G.: Deep anomaly detection with outlier exposure. arXiv preprint arXiv:1812.04606 (2018)
20. Huberman, B.A., Franklin, M., Hogg, T.: Enhancing privacy and trust in electronic communities. In: Proceedings of the 1st ACM Conference on Electronic Commerce, pp. 78–86. ACM (1999)
21. IDC: Smartphone OS market share (2017). https://www.idc.com/promo/smartphone-market-share/os
22. Kiss, Á., Liu, J., Schneider, T., Asokan, N., Pinkas, B.: Private set intersection for unequal set sizes with mobile applications. Proc. Priv. Enhancing Technol. **2017**(4), 177–197 (2017)
23. KQED Science: Scientists looked at DNA supposedly from a Yeti and here's what they found, December 2017. https://goo.gl/uDvypP
24. Lee, J., Clifton, C.: How much is enough? Choosing ε for differential privacy. In: Lai, X., Zhou, J., Li, H. (eds.) ISC 2011. LNCS, vol. 7001, pp. 325–340. Springer, Heidelberg (2011). https://doi.org/10.1007/978-3-642-24861-0_22
25. Malkhi, D., Nisan, N., Pinkas, B., Sella, Y., et al.: Fairplay-secure two-party computation system. In: USENIX Security Symposium (2004)
26. McGillion, B., Dettenborn, T., Nyman, T., Asokan, N.: Open-TEE-an open virtual trusted execution environment. In: 2015 IEEE Trustcom/BigDataSE/ISPA, vol. 1, pp. 400–407. IEEE (2015)
27. McSherry, F.D.: Privacy integrated queries: an extensible platform for privacy-preserving data analysis. In: Proceedings of the 2009 ACM SIGMOD International Conference on Management of Data, pp. 19–30. ACM (2009)
28. Miller, A., Hicks, M., Katz, J., Shi, E.: Authenticated data structures, generically. In: ACM SIGPLAN Notices, vol. 49, pp. 411–423. ACM (2014)
29. Miller, R.B.: Response time in man-computer conversational transactions. In: Proceedings of the December 9–11, 1968, Fall Joint Computer Conference, Part I, pp. 267–277. ACM (1968)
30. Minitab: Proceed with the analysis if the sample is large enough (2020). https://support.minitab.com/en-us/minitab/19/help-and-how-to/statistics/basic-statistics/supporting-topics/normality/what-to-do-with-nonnormal-data/
31. MOCACARE: Blood pressure monitor (2020). https://www.mocacare.com/mocacuff/
32. Mohan, P., Thakurta, A., Shi, E., Song, D., Culler, D.: GUPT: privacy preserving data analysis made easy. In: Proceedings of the 2012 ACM SIGMOD International Conference on Management of Data, pp. 349–360. ACM (2012)

33. Mohassel, P., Franklin, M.: Efficiency tradeoffs for malicious two-party computation. In: Yung, M., Dodis, Y., Kiayias, A., Malkin, T. (eds.) PKC 2006. LNCS, vol. 3958, pp. 458–473. Springer, Heidelberg (2006). https://doi.org/10.1007/11745853_30

34. Nguyen, N.: A lot of apps sell your data. here's what you can do about it (2018). https://www.buzzfeednews.com/article/nicolenguyen/how-apps-take-your-data-and-sell-it-without-you-even

35. Omron: Omron wearable blood pressure monitor (2020). https://omronhealthcare.com/products/heartguide-wearable-blood-pressure-monitor-bp8000m/

36. O'Sullivan, D.: Cloud leak: how a Verizon partner exposed millions of customer accounts (2017). https://www.upguard.com/breaches/verizon-cloud-leak

37. Pang, G., Cao, L., Chen, L., Liu, H.: Unsupervised feature selection for outlier detection by modelling hierarchical value-feature couplings. In: 2016 IEEE 16th International Conference on Data Mining (ICDM), pp. 410–419. IEEE (2016)

38. Paverd, A., Martin, A., Brown, I.: Modelling and automatically analysing privacy properties for honest-but-curious adversaries. Technical report (2014)

39. Roy, I., Setty, S.T.V., Kilzer, A., Shmatikov, V., Witchel, E.: Airavat: security and privacy for MapReduce. In: Proceedings of the 7th USENIX Conference on Networked Systems Design and Implementation, NSDI 2010, p. 20. USENIX Association, Berkeley (2010). http://dl.acm.org/citation.cfm?id=1855711.1855731

40. Singer, N.: New data rules could empower patients but undermine their privacy (2020). https://www.nytimes.com/2020/03/09/technology/medical-app-patients-data-privacy.html

41. Statt, N.: Some major android apps are still sending data directly to Facebook (2019). https://www.theverge.com/2019/3/5/18252397/facebook-android-apps-sending-data-user-privacy-developer-tools-violation

42. F. Marketing Team: How much money can you earn with an app in 2019 (2019). https://fueled.com/blog/much-money-can-earn-app/

43. The New Daily: Federal government to force tech giants to reveal user data (2018). https://thenewdaily.com.au/news/national/2018/08/14/tech-surveillance-laws/

44. Vallina-Rodriguez, N., et al.: When David helps goliath: the case for 3G onloading. In: Proceedings of the 11th ACM Workshop on Hot Topics in Networks, pp. 85–90. ACM (2012)

45. VARONIS: 2018 VARONIS global data risk report (2018). https://www.varonis.com/2018-data-risk-report/

46. Vu, X.S., Jiang, L.: Self-adaptive privacy concern detection for user-generated content. arXiv preprint arXiv:1806.07221 (2018)

47. Wendt, N., Julien, C.: PACO: a system-level abstraction for on-loading contextual data to mobile devices. IEEE Trans. Mob. Comput. **17**(9), 2127–2140 (2018)

Service Performance Analysis of Cloud Computing Server by Queuing System

Ruijuan Wang[1], Guangjun Zai[1(✉)], Yan Liu[2,3], and Haibo Pang[1]

[1] School of Software, Zhengzhou University, Zhengzhou, China
zaiguangjun@zzu.edu.cn
[2] School of Mathematics and Statistics, Zhengzhou University, Zhengzhou, China
[3] Henan Key Laboratory of Financial Engineering, Zhengzhou, China

Abstract. Performance analysis of cloud computing server provides the basis for ensuring Quality of Service (QoS), and the service strategy of server will directly affect the analysis of performance indicators. The performance indicators of QoS are usually defined in the form of Service Layer Agreement (SLA), such as the average response time, the average queue length, immediate service probability and so on. In this work, Service performance analysis models based on $Geo/G/1$ queuing system and queuing system with the vacation of the server are proposed. In these models, we analyze the main performance indicators of cloud computing server for the different parameters: the time between arrive of the task, the time of service, and the time of the provision of vacation. Furthermore, we discuss the optimizing concurrent number of the cloud computing.

Keywords: $Geo/G/1$ queuing system · Cloud computing · Performance analysis · Response time

1 Introduction

Cloud computing is the further development of distributed computing, parallel processing and grid computing, and quickly becomes a hot spot in industry and academic research [1, 2]. QoS performance metrics typically includes response time, blocking probability and probability of immediate service. If the cloud computing center is assumed to be a random service system, each computing resource (e.g., network server, database server) can be deemed as a service platform. To build a stochastic service system, the QoS performance metrics can be discussed by the research method of queuing theory.

The performance indicators of QoS are usually defined in the form of Service Layer Agreement (SLA). SLA is a consultative agreement between customers and service providers, including service availability, performance, and data protection and security [3]. Accurate prediction of customer service needs can enable service providers to avoid over provisioning resources in order to satisfy SLA. Customer request is a variable load. It is difficult to satisfy SLA and achieve optimal utilization of resources by dynamically

© ICST Institute for Computer Sciences, Social Informatics and Telecommunications Engineering 2022
Published by Springer Nature Switzerland AG 2022. All Rights Reserved
S. Deng et al. (Eds.): MobiCASE 2021, LNICST 434, pp. 42–53, 2022.
https://doi.org/10.1007/978-3-030-99203-3_3

configuring computing resources [4]. However, we can analyze the service performance by modeling the cloud computing center, and obtain the probability distribution of the request response time and other performance indicators, and discuss the factors that affect the performance of the cloud computing center.

At present, the use of queuing theory calculation service performance analysis and modeling centers on the cloud technology research work is very little to this theory research. In 2012, KHAZAEI H et al. [5] used the M/G/m queuing model to analyze the relationship between the average response time, average queue length and the number of service station. B. Yang et al. [6] in 2009 and H. W. He et al. [7] in 2014 proposed the approximate analysis model of computing center of M/M/n/n+r queuing system based on the cloud, which obtained the user request response distribution function of time and other important performance metrics QoS through solving the model. K. Q. Xiong provided a M/M/1 Queuing System, which was a response time model for servers providing Web services. The probability distribution of the response time and its mean value are given [8]. In 2013, H. Wang set up a set of mapping rules that mapped the various "internal causes" and "external causes" affecting the performance of Web services to G/G/1 FCFS, M/G/1 PS and M/G/ infinity queuing nodes. Further more, he gave a group of Web services based on the queuing network and proposed the combination of performance analysis index system and its calculation formula [9].

In a queuing system, service stations will adopt various strategies of customer reception in some time, and this service is temporarily interrupted time (usually is random variable) is referred to the vacation. In 2015, we presented a queuing system part of the service station based on asynchronous multiple vacation and the service process of cloud computing center corresponding queuing system, by the analysis of the corresponding queuing model, to investigate the performance index and optimize the allocation of resources in cloud computing [10].

2 Cloud Computing Server Queuing System Model

The user sends task to the cloud computing center and a suitable computing node provides service. After service completes, the task leaves. Compute node contains different computing resources, such as network server, database server. The assumption of a computing node corresponds to queuing service of one system, the user sends the corresponding queuing system task arrival process, user services complete the service process corresponding to the queuing system, the process of resource allocation in cloud computing server can correspond to a queue model.

So the process of resource allocation in cloud computing server may correspond to a part of the queuing system $Geo/G/1$ [11, 12].

(i)   The time between arrive of the task is time series $\{\tau_k, k = 1, 2, \cdots\}$, and τ_k is independent and identical distribution (i.i.d.). The distribution of τ_k is the Geometric Distribution with the parameter p,

$$P\{\tau = j\} = p(1 - p)^{j-1}, j = 1, 2, \cdots, 0 < p < 1$$

(ii) In the system there is one server, and the time of service is variable χ. The distribution of χ is a Discrete Distributions

$$P\{\chi = j\} = g_j, j = 1, 2, \cdots$$

Cumulative distribution function of service time is $G(j)$, and the Probability generating function is.

$$G^*(z) = \sum_{j=1}^{\infty} g_j z^j, |z| < 1$$

And the average service time per request is $\mu(1 \leq \mu < \infty)$. Customer service according to FCFS service rules.

(iii) The arrival time and the service time are independent.

The variable $N(n)$ is the number of customer in the service system, that is, queue length of the queuing system. Supposing $\rho = p\mu$ is the traffic intensity of the service system, and $\bar{p} = 1 - p$. We can analyze the quality of service by a discrete time $Geo/G/1$ Queuing service system.

3 Model Analysis and Service Performance Metrics by $Geo/G/1$

The $N(n)$ represents the task numbers in the cloud computing system at the time of n, and distribution of steady queue length

$$p_j = \lim_{n \to \infty} P\{N(n) = j\}, j = 0, 1, 2, \cdots$$

(i) when $\rho \geq 1, p_j = 0, j = 0, 1, 2, \cdots$.

(ii) when $\rho < 1$, the recursion expressions of $\{p_j, j = 0, 1, 2, \cdots\}$ for the transient queue length distribution is [12]

$$p_0 = 1 - \rho,$$

$$p_1 = \frac{(1 - \rho)(1 - G^*(\bar{p}))}{G^*(\bar{p})},$$

$$p_j = \frac{1}{G^*(\bar{p})} \left\{ p(1 - \rho) \sum_{n=j-1}^{\infty} \sum_{k=n+1}^{\infty} g_k \binom{n}{j-1} p^{j-1} \bar{p}^{n-j+1} \right.$$

$$\left. + \sum_{i=1}^{j-1} p_{j-i} \left(1 - G^*(\bar{p}) - \sum_{m=1}^{i} \sum_{k=m}^{\infty} g_k \binom{k}{m} p^m \bar{p}^{k-m} \right) \right\}, j = 2, 3, \cdots$$

where $j \leq 0, \sum_{i=1}^{j} = 0$.

This is related to service performance index of cloud computing center.

(1) **The probability of immediate service**
If a customer arrives and the existence of station service is free, customer service can be accepted immediately without waiting. The probability of this happening calls immediate service probability. By the teady queue length distribution, it is immediate service probability that can be got:

$$p_0 = 1 - \rho.$$

(2) **The time of the server idle**
The server idle is the time when the system has just turned empty until the time when a customer arrives. Supposing the variable $\hat{\tau}$ is the server idle, we can get that the $\hat{\tau}$ is the Geometric distribution

$$P\{\hat{\tau} = j\} = p(1-p)^{j-1}, \quad j = 1, 2, \cdots, 0 < p < 1$$

And the server busy period is the time when the system has a customer arrives until the time when the last customer leaves, expressed by variable b. Average time of continuous work of cloud computing server is the expectation of b, and its value is

$$E[b] = \begin{cases} \frac{\rho}{p(1-\rho)}, & \rho < 1, \\ \infty, & \rho \geq 1. \end{cases}$$

(3) **Average number of clients waiting for service on the server (total system request)**
According to the definition of the expectations, average number of clients waiting for service on the server is the average queue length $E[N]$ of the queuing system (the number of requests for queuing):

$$E[N] = \rho + \frac{p^2}{2(1-\rho)} E\left[\chi^2 - \chi\right],$$

where $E\left[\chi^2\right] = \sum_{j=1}^{\infty} j^2 g_j$.

(4) **The distribution of response time**
The sum of queue waiting time and accepting the service time is called the request response time. They are mutually independent. In the queuing model, the waiting time can be calculated by the following ways.

When $\rho < 1$, the waiting time $W(t)$ can be decomposed into the sum of all service time of requests for queuing in $Geo/G/1$ queuing system. The distribution of $W(t)$ is

$$H_W(t) = \sum_{j=0}^{\infty} p_j \times G^{(j+1)}(t),$$

where $G^{(j)}(t)$ is the j-Fold Convolution of $G(t)$.

(5) **The average response time**

The average response time of requests is the sum of the average waiting time of customers and the average business hours of customers in queuing system, so the average response time $T = E[W]$, That is,

$$T = E[W] = E[N] \times E[\chi]$$

$$= \mu \left(\rho + \frac{p^2}{2(1-\rho)} E\left[\chi^2 - \chi\right] \right).$$

4 Service Performance Metrics by *Geo/G/1* with the Vacation

In practical application, a service cloud computing server may interrupt occurs. On the other hand, in order to optimize the service system and improve the system of economic benefit, the relative leisure time server is to engage in other work. The vacation policy can provide great flexibility for the design and optimization of process control system. So when the cloud computing center operates computing resources in the dynamic configuration, the vacation of the server is needed to be considered to achieve the optimal allocation of resources utilization. Because the queue system with a variety of vacation policy is complex, the study and calculation of indicators is difficult. So the research on QoS performance of current did not consider the vacation of service station.

In a queuing system, service stations will adopt various strategies of customer reception in some time, this service is temporarily interrupted time (usually is random variable) is referred to the vacation. This paper presents a queuing system, in which part of the service station is based on asynchronous multiple vacation, and the service process of cloud computing center corresponds to queuing system, and by the analysis of the corresponding queuing model, investigates the performance index and optimizes the allocation of resources in cloud computing.

The user sends the cloud computing task for service in a suitable computing node. After service is completed, the task leaves. Computing node contains different computing resources, such as network server, database server. The assumption of a computing node corresponds to queuing service of one system, the corresponding queuing system task arrival process which the user sends and the service process corresponding to the queuing system which user services complete, can be the process of resource allocation in Cloud Computing corresponds to a queue model. The real cloud computing services is generally part of server vacation leave, leave for asynchronous start, and in the absence of the user can be repeatedly leave. So the process of resource allocation in cloud computing center may correspond to a part of the service station asynchronous multiple vacation queuing system *Geo/G/1* [13, 14].

The system model discussed in this paper, the following specific vacation policy:

(1) The time of task arrival interval is time series $\{\tau_k, k = 1, 2, \cdots\}$, and τ_k is i.i.d. The distribution of τ_k is the Geometric Distribution with the parameter p,

$$P\{\tau = j\} = p(1-p)^{j-1}, j = 1, 2, \cdots, 0 < p < 1;$$

(2) In the system there is one service station, and the time of service is variable χ. The distribution of χ is a Discrete Distributions

$$P\{\chi = j\} = g_j, j = 1, 2, \cdots$$

Customer service according to FCFS service rules;

(3) A service platform not only can complete a customer service system and meet in the customer waiting, but also can continue for the next customer service.

(4) When there is no customers waiting for service in the system, the service station will be in the provision of vacation. If the customers arrive in the time of the provision of vacation, the service station must begin to service. If there are not customers in the time of the provision of vacation, the service station starts the vacation.

The time of the provision of vacation is random variable Y with the Discrete Distributions

$$P\{Y = j\} = y_j, j = 0, 1, 2, \cdots$$

Cumulative distribution function of provision time is $Y(j)$, and the Probability generating function is $Y^*(z) = \sum_{j=1}^{\infty} y_j z^j, |z| < 1$, and the average provision time is $E(Y)$.

(5) A service station vacation is continue, if the system is still no customers waiting for service, or the number of customer is less than N_0.

(6) If the number of the customer in the system is more than N_0, then the service station vacation is end. In particular, when the first customer of the system arrives, the service station starts the service immediately.

(7) The arrival time, the service time and the provision time are independent.

So we can analyze the quality of service by a discrete time $Geo/G/1$ Queuing service system with vacation.

The steady distribution of the task number in the cloud computing system is $p_j = \lim_{n \to \infty} P\{N(n) = j\}, j = 0, 1, 2, \cdots$,

(i) when $\rho \geq 1, p_j = 0, j = 0, 1, 2, \cdots$;

(ii) when $\rho < 1$, the recursion expressions of $\{p_j, j = 0, 1, 2, \cdots\}$ for the transient queue length distribution is [14, 15]

$$p_0 = \frac{1 - \rho}{1 + (N_0 - 1)Y(\overline{p})},$$

$$p_j = p_0 \left\{ p\theta_j + Y(\overline{p}) + pY(\overline{p}) \sum_{k=1}^{j-1} \theta_k \right\}, j = 1, 2, \cdots, N_0 - 1,$$

$$p_j = pp_0 \left\{ \theta_j + Y(\overline{p}) \sum_{k=1}^{N-1} \theta_{j-N+k} \right\}, j = N_0, N_0 + 1, \cdots$$

where $j \leq 0$, $\sum_{i=1}^{j} = 0$,

$$\theta_1 = \frac{1 - G^*(\overline{p})}{pG^*(\overline{p})},$$

$$\theta_j = \frac{1}{G^*(\overline{p})} \left\{ \sum_{n=j-1}^{\infty} \sum_{k=n+1}^{\infty} g_k \binom{n}{j-1} p^{j-1} \overline{p}^{n-j+1} \right.$$
$$\left. + \sum_{i=1}^{j-1} \theta_{j-i} \left[1 - G^*(\overline{p}) - \sum_{m=1}^{i} \sum_{k=m}^{\infty} \binom{k}{m} g_k p^m \overline{p}^{k-m} \right] \right\} \quad j = 2, 3, \cdots$$

So this can be related to service performance index of cloud computing.

(1) **The time of the service busy**

The variable b is the server busy period, and the Probability generating function of the variable b is $B^*(z) = \sum_{j=1}^{\infty} P\{b = j\}z^j$, $|z| < 1$ and $B^*(z) = G^*((\overline{p} + pB^*(z))z)$. The expectation of b is

$$E[b] = \begin{cases} \frac{\rho}{p(1-\rho)}, & \rho < 1, \\ \infty, & \rho \geq 1. \end{cases}$$

(2) **Average number of clients waiting for service on the server**

According to the definition of the expectations, Average time of continuous work of cloud computing server is the average queue length $E[N]$ of the queuing system (the number of requests for queuing):

$$E[N] = \rho + \frac{p^2}{2(1-\rho)} E[\chi^2 - \chi] + \frac{Y(\overline{p})}{1 + (N_0 - 1)Y(\overline{p})} \times \frac{N_0(N_0 - 1)}{2},$$

where $E[\chi^2] = \sum_{j=1}^{\infty} j^2 g_j$.

(3) **The distribution of requests for queuing number**

The Probability generating function of the number of the queuing task variable N in the cloud computing system is $\pi(z) = \sum_{j=0}^{\infty} p_j z^j$, $|z| < 1$.

When $\rho < 1$, we have

$$\pi(z) = \frac{(1-\rho)(1-z)G^*(\overline{p} + pz)}{G^*(\overline{p} + pz) - z} \times \frac{1 - z + Y(\overline{p})(z - z^N)}{(1-z)[1 + (N_0 - 1)Y(\overline{p})]}.$$

(4) The average response time

The average response time of requests is the sum of the average waiting time and average business hours in queuing system for customers. So the average response time $T = E[W]$, That is,

$$T = E[W] \geq E[N] \times E[\chi]$$

$$= \mu \left(\rho + \frac{p^2}{2(1-\rho)} E\left[\chi^2 - \chi\right] + \frac{Y(\bar{p})}{1+(N_0-1)Y(\bar{p})} \times \frac{N_0(N_0-1)}{2} \right).$$

5   Model Analysis and Service Performance Index

Assuming that the system simulation time in minutes, the arrival interval of task obeys the Geometric Distribution with $p = 0.2$, the service completion time obeys the Discrete Distributions with $\mu = 2$. We can analyze service performance index of the cloud computing system.

5.1   Service Performance Index with no Vacation

(1) The immediate service probability is

$$p_0 = 1 - \rho = 1 - p\mu = 0.6.$$

(2) The expectation of the server busy period is

$$E[b] = \frac{\rho}{p(1-\rho)} = 0.3333.$$

(3) The steady distribution of the queuing task p_j is in the Table 1:

Table 1. The stead distribution of the queuing task

	p_0	p_1	p_2	p_3	p_4	p_4
Probability	0.8523	0.1094	0.0268	0.0083	0.0015	0.0006

(4) Average number of clients waiting for service on the server

$$E[N] = 0.1971$$

(5) The average response time is

$$T = E[W] = E[N] \times E[\chi] = 0.3942.$$

5.2   Service Performance Index with Vacation

The time of the provision of vacation is variable Y that is the Geometric Distribution with parameter q. The number of the customer in the system is more than N_0, then the service station vacation is end.

(1) When $p = 0.2, \mu = 2, N_0 = 5$, we discuss the stead distribution of the queuing task at $q = 0.01, or\, q = 0.1, or\, q = 0.3$, such as Fig. 1.

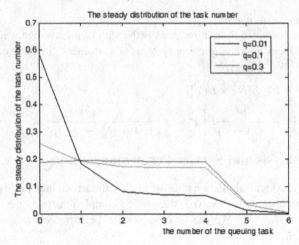

Fig. 1. The stead distribution of the queuing task at $q = 0.01, or\ q = 0.1, or\ q = 0.3$.

By the stead distribution, we can calculate the average number of queuing task in the Table 2.

Table 2. The average number of clients waiting for service on the server by q.

	$q = 0.01$	$q = 0.1$	$q = 0.3$
The average number of clients waiting for service on the server	0.89	1.92	2.14

(2) When $p = 0.2$, $\mu = 2$, $q = 0.05$, we discuss the stead distribution of the queuing task at $N_0 = 1$, $or\ N_0 = 3$, $or\ N_0 = 5$, such as Fig. 2.

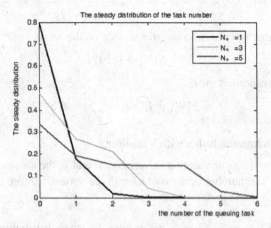

Fig. 2. The stead distribution of the queuing task at $N_0 = 1$, $or\ N_0 = 3$, $or\ N_0 = 5$.

By the stead distribution, we can calculate the average number of clients waiting for service on the server in the Table 3.

Table 3. The average number of clients waiting for service on the server by N_0.

	$N_0 = 1$	$N_0 = 3$	$N_0 = 5$
Average number of clients waiting for service on the server	0.23	0.84	1.67

(3) When $N_0 = 5$, $\mu = 2$, $q = 0.05$, we discuss the stead distribution of the queuing task at $p = 0.01$, or $p = 0.05$, or $p = 0.2$, or $p = 0.4$, such as Fig. 3.

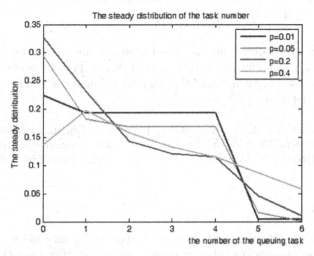

Fig. 3. The stead distribution of the queuing task at $p = 0.01$, or $p = 0.05$, or $p = 0.2$, or $p = 0.4$.

By the stead distribution, we can calculate Average number of clients waiting for service on the server in the Table 4.

Table 4. The average number of clients waiting for service on the server by p.

	$p = 0.01$	$p = 0.05$	$p = 0.2$	$p = 0.4$
The average number of clients waiting for service on the server	1.95	1.78	1.67	3.2

5.3 Optimizing Concurrent Number of the Cloud Computing

The concurrent number of the cloud computing is not enough to be more than the mean. For example, when $p = 0.2, \mu = 2, N_0 = 5, q = 0.05$, the stead distribution of the queuing task is in the Table 5.

Table 5. The stead distribution of the queuing task

	p_0	p_1	p_2	p_3	p_4	p_5	p_6	p_7
Probability	0.3362	0.1907	0.1500	0.1455	0.1450	0.0290	0.0032	0.0004

In this system, the average number of queuing task is 1.67. So

$$P\{N > E(N)\} = P\{N > 1.67\} \approx 0.373.$$

That is, the Probability of the concurrent number is not enough which is 37.3% if the concurrent number is the mean of queuing task. For the Probability of the concurrent is enough which will be greater than 99%, we must get the concurrent number which is more than 6 $(p_0 + p_1 + p_2 + \cdots + p_6 > 99\%)$.

Acknowledgement. The thesis is supported by Postgraduate Education Reform and Quality Improvement Project of Henan Province (YJS2021AL008). I shall extend my thanks to Yan Liu for all his kindness and help. I'd like to thank my school for providing the experimental environment.

References

1. Buyya, R., Yeo, C.S., Venugopal, S., et al.: Cloud computing and e-merging IT platforms: vision, hype, and reality for delivering computing as the 5th utility. Futur. Gener. Comput. Syst. **25**(6), 599–616 (2009)
2. Zhang, Q., Cheng, L., Boutaba, R.: Cloud computing: state-of-the-art and research challenges. J. Internet Serv. Appl. **1**(1), 7–18 (2010). https://doi.org/10.1007/s13174-010-0007-6
3. Patel, P., Ranabahu, A.H., Sheth, A.P.: Service level agreement in cloud computing [C/OL] (2013). http://knoesis.wright.edu/library/download/OOPSLA_cloud_wsla_v3.pdf
4. Xiong, K., Perros, H.: Service performance and analysis in cloud computing. In: Proceedings of the 2009 World Conference on Services, pp. 693–700. IEEE, Piscataway (2009)
5. Khazaei, H., Misic, J., Misic, V.B.: Performance analysis of cloud computing centers using m/g/m/m+r queueing systems. IEEE Trans. Parallel Distrib. Syst. **23**(5), 936–943 (2012)
6. Yang, B., Tan, F., Dai, Yuan-Shun., Guo, S.: Performance evaluation of cloud service considering fault recovery. In: Jaatun, M.G., Zhao, G., Rong, C. (eds.) CloudCom 2009. LNCS, vol. 5931, pp. 571–576. Springer, Heidelberg (2009). https://doi.org/10.1007/978-3-642-10665-1_54
7. He, H., Fu, Y., Yang, Y., Xiao, T.: Service performance analysis of cloud computing center based on M/M/n/n + r queueing model. J. Comput. Appl. **34**(7), 1843–1847 (2014)
8. Xiong, K.: Web services performance modeling and analysis. In: Proceeding of the 6th International Symposium on High Capacity Optical Networks and Enabling Technologies, Alexandria, Egypt, pp. 1–6 (2009)

9. Wang, H., Huang, M.-H., Long, H.: The performance analysis of web services composition based on queueing network with G/G/1-FCFS, M/G/1-PS and M/G/∞ Nodes. Chin. J. Comput. **36**(1), 22–38 (2014). https://doi.org/10.3724/SP.J.1016.2013.00022

10. Zai, G., Liuyan: Service performance analysis of cloud computing center based on vacation Queueing system. J. Comput. Inf. Syst. **11**(19) 7029–7036 (2015)

11. Tian, N.S.: Stochastic service systems with vacations. Peking University Press, Beijing, pp. 299–315 (2001)

12. Tang, Y.: Queueing Theory: Basic and Analytical Techniques. Science Press, Beijing (2006)

13. Tang, Y.: Queue-length distribution and capacity optimum design for Geo/G/1 queueing system with delayed N-policy and set-up time. Math. Appl. **24**(3), 567–574 (2011)

14. Wei, Y.-Y., Tang, Y.-H., Gu, J.-X.: Queue length distribution and numerical calculation for Geo/G/1 Queueing system with delayed N-policy. Syst. Eng.-Theory Pract. **31**(11), 2151–2160 (2013)

15. Wei, Y.-Y., Tang, Y.-H., Gu, J.-X.: Queue size distribution and capacity optimum design for Geo/G/1 queueing system with delayed D-policy. **33**(4), 996–1005 (2013)

CLES: A Universal Wrench
for Embedded Systems Communication
and Coordination

Jason Davis$^{(\boxtimes)}$ and Eli Tilevich

Software Innovations Lab, Virginia Tech, Blacksburg, USA
{jdvavis7,tilevich}@vt.edu

Abstract. Modern embedded systems—autonomous vehicle-to-vehicle communication, smart cities, and military Joint All-Domain Operations—feature increasingly heterogeneous distributed components. As a result, existing communication methods, tightly coupled with specific networking layers and individual applications, can no longer balance the flexibility of modern data distribution with the traditional constraints of embedded systems. To address this problem, this paper presents a domain-specific language, designed around the Representational State Transfer (REST) architecture, most famously used on the web. Our language, called the Communication Language for Embedded Systems (CLES), supports both traditional point-to-point data communication and allocation of decentralized distributed tasks. To meet the traditional constraints of embedded execution, CLES's novel runtime allocates decentralized distributed tasks across a heterogeneous network of embedded devices, overcoming limitations of centralized management and limited operating system integration. We evaluated CLES with performance micro-benchmarks, implementation of distributed stochastic gradient descent, and by applying it to design versatile stateless services for vehicle-to-vehicle communication and military Joint All-Domain Command and Control, thus meeting the data distribution needs of realistic cyber-physical embedded systems.

Keywords: Embedded networking · Low-latency networking · Vehicle to vehicle communication · RESTful architecture

1 Introduction

Modern embedded systems are increasingly heterogeneous, collaborative, and networked. Disparate systems, each with its own computing architecture, operating system, and purpose, coordinate with each other to achieve a common goal. Their communication and coordination functionality is provided via a custom, highly optimized specialized protocol for each pair of connected systems. For safety-critical cyber-physical systems, this approach is deemed as required to meet the timeliness requirements. Unfortunately, the resulting low-level, platform-specific code is hard to write, extend, and maintain.

© ICST Institute for Computer Sciences, Social Informatics and Telecommunications Engineering 2022
Published by Springer Nature Switzerland AG 2022. All Rights Reserved
S. Deng et al. (Eds.): MobiCASE 2021, LNICST 434, pp. 54–68, 2022.
https://doi.org/10.1007/978-3-030-99203-3_4

Web development coordinates heterogeneous distributed components via the RESTful architectural style [6] with its ubiquitous HTTP communication, while high-powered computing manages distributed workloads with container orchestration platforms, such as Docker Swarm and Kubernetes. Unfortunately, developers cannot apply these proven solutions to distributed embedded systems, with their proprietary architectures, operating system limitations, centralized management requirements, and non-deterministic timing constraints.

To support the creation of heterogeneous networked solutions easily integrated into embedded systems, this paper presents CLES[1], a Domain Specific Language (DSL) for implementing simple, stateless, communication protocols in the RESTful architectural style [6]. With its simple syntax and platform APIs, CLES keeps the complexity of networking architecture and protocols abstracted from the application developer, thus providing a flexible and robust communication mechanism, designed to minimize the required learning curve and development burden. Designed to meet the communication and coordination requirements of embedded systems, CLES is implemented in standard C++. CLES integrates point-to-point communication to maintain deterministic timeliness constraints, interfacing with the OSI Internet Protocol (IP) network stack instead of low-level wireless protocols for flexibility. CLES also provides a powerful runtime that meets advanced distributed computing requirements, such as decentralized task allocation.

This paper makes the following contributions:

- *An application of the RESTful architecture for the communication and coordination needs of modern embedded systems.* We demonstrate how the proven benefits of REST, including first-class support for heterogeneity, uniformity, and simplicity, can be extended to embedded systems, without sacrificing this domain's timeliness constraints.
- *CLES—a platform independent DSL with supporting SDK and runtime for implementing RESTful architecture's communication and coordination in embedded systems.* The CLES runtime introduces novel asymmetric task registration and remote access, in order to meet the unique execution constraints of its target domain.
- *An empirical evaluation of CLES with representative performance microbenchmarks, a reference distributed stochastic gradient descent implementation, and realistic case studies.*

2   Problem Domain: Embedded Distributed Computing

Both the automotive and defense industries are paving the way for large-scale, decentralized distributed computing systems. The defining characteristics of their distributed networks are dynamic connectivity graphs, heterogeneous systems, real-time operating systems, low-power devices, decentralized requirements, high reliability, and limited bandwidth. Kubernetes is currently being

---

[1] CLES stands for **C**ommunication **L**anguage for **E**mbedded **S**ystems.

explored as a solution for both the U.S. Air Force [7] and the automotive industry. Kubernetes and other Container Orchestration solutions are not ideal for
this problem space, as they are typically centralized, limited to non-real-time OS,
inapplicable to hardware-integrated platforms (e.g., FPGA data processing), and
lacking non-container interfaces into the distributed processing network.

2.1   Use Case: Vehicle Platooning

A fundamental challenge of autonomous vehicles and vehicle to everything (V2X)
communication is vehicle platooning. *An automated vehicle platoon* is a series of
vehicles, most notably trucks, that maintain a group (platoon) on the highway,
with a software control module controlling each vehicle's steering and speed.
With its constituent vehicles communicating and coordinating with each other,
a platoon increases the safety and energy efficiency of highway travel [9].

A traditional Vehicle to Vehicle (V2V) communication problem, platooning
is constrained by networking challenges and algorithmic design. Notably, 802.11p
and 5G are the two proven network solutions that satisfy the minimum requirements for latency, reliability, and security for vehicle platooning [1]. Additionally,
Swaroop [10], Arefizadeh [9], and Liangyi [11] introduced algorithms that defined
the minimum data transmission required to achieve stable platoons. One question that remains unexplored is what kind of software architecture and abstrac-
tions are needed to realize practical platooning solutions (Fig. 1).

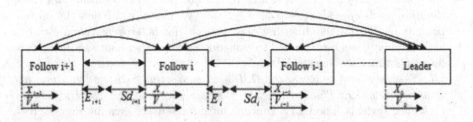

Fig. 1. Platooning networking structure [10]

As baseline networking protocols, our implementation references 802.11p and
5G, which both support OSI IP [8] and uses the defined minimum dataset
required for stable platooning: lead vehicle localization data (UTC Time, latitude, longitude, Velocity, and Acceleration), and immediately ahead vehicle
localization [10].

Traditional Challenges. The traditional methods for point-to-point communication involve either defining a transmission via an inflexible, interface control
document (ICD) serialized packet, or defining the data structure within the
data-link layer itself, such as in military communications Link-16 and MADL.

In this use case, the traditional approach that integrates the communication
functionality directly into the data link layer increases development time, reduces

flexibility for enhancements, hinders upgradability, and complicates integration with other wireless solutions. Using an ICD defined serialized packet for transmission suffers from similar limitations. The time to market for this solution can be very quick, and the integration time is minimal, but the ICD's restricted structure of the packet definition heavily constrains flexibility and upgradability. More modern solutions for this data distribution problem include ActiveMQ and DDS. However, ActiveMQ requires a centralized data broker. While DDS is decentralized, DDS requires a significant development effort to properly support vehicle to vehicle communication, as data middleware without high-level language bindings. Lastly, common real-time OS' VxWorks and QNX provides no support for Kubernetes, removing it from consideration.

2.2   Use Case: Joint All-Domain Command and Control (JDAC)

One of the core design requirements for the U.S. Military Joint All-Domain Command and Control (JDAC) is integration of heterogeneous assets to form a distributed sensor network that both informs decision makers and improves strike capabilities [4]. JDAC includes heterogeneous, distributed sensor networks, in which devices have a wide range of computing power and specialized hardware. These networks must efficiently distribute processing tasks across multiple devices for real-time situational awareness.

For the purpose of demonstrating the core challenges required to meet this goal, we construct an example concept of operations (CONOPS). This CONOPS includes two different aircraft, one satellite, and a mission operations center. The first aircraft is a reconnaissance unmanned aircraft, equipped with an Electro-Optical/Infra-Red (EO/IR) camera capable of sending encoded Full Motion Video (FMV). The second aircraft is an fighter jet capable of launching a ground strike. The satellite hosts a powerful processor, machine learning algorithms, and other sources of data for fusion.

For the network architecture the satellite only has a data link to the reconnaissance aircraft. Both aircraft can communicate through data links with the mission center, but not with each other. This sparsely connected graph of connectivity reasonably represents a realistic scenario with modern proprietary, incompatible data links in the U.S. Air Force.

The first operational requirement for the reconnaissance aircraft is to collect FMV and route the data stream to the satellite for machine learning driven processing. The satellite returns a "Track" for all targets synthesized from the data. The reconnaissance aircraft sends Track information to the mission control station. The mission control station enables officers to make informed decisions. Finally, the operation lead sends a strike command to the strike aircraft, with the associated Track from the satellite/reconnaissance aircraft fusion. The final result is a more accurate strike achieved by fusing the supplied Track with data on-board the strike vehicle. More importantly, the decision to strike can be made quickly and confidently by reducing the data-to-decision time provided by the sensor network integrated ground station.

Traditional Challenges. The traditional approach to developing this sort of joint operation would involve each primary contractor for the different platforms to develop custom interfaces between each asset. These interfaces would require long development and test cycles, and commonly be too specific to allow for re-usability as this network is expanded to support additional aircraft.

Existing Approach. The CONOPS proposed above is similar to the design drivers cited for the U-2 Kubernetes integration [7]. Although Kubernetes is a powerful tool for distributing tasks via container orchestration, it is limited to certain OS. Only some of the highly heterogeneous participating assets in a Joint All-Domain Operation can host Kubernetes.

3 RESTful Architecture for Distributed Embedded Systems

Our Communication Language for Embedded systems (CLES) and Software Development Kit (SDK) support a broad problem space with a wide variety of inter-process and inter-device scenarios, while overcoming some of the most salient constraints of embedded systems development. Incidentally *clé[s]* is "wrench" in French, and our objective has been to create a universal wrench for communication and coordination in embedded systems.

For low latency point-to-point communications, we argue that a RESTful request and response communication model, similar to the ubiquitous Java net.http package, can offer a more flexible point-to-point alternative that meets the same execution requirements. For distributed workloads, our approach supports decentralized, asymmetric, task allocation through simple portable C++ plugins loaded by a standalone runtime.

3.1 Requirements

Distributing an application across devices removes the applicability of all inter-process communication within an OS, such as shared memory, memory mapped I/O, pipes, OS messaging, semaphores, etc. The next descriptor of system requirements is *heterogeneity*: systems running on any hardware or OS should be able to interface with the communication functionality.

The example problem of a sensor network implies that the network consists of at least some nodes that are highly specialized, possibly low-powered devices with an array of sensors. These devices need to maintain their network coordination with *minimal overhead* and software.

The final key requirement to consider is *decentralized*. In our problem domain, one cannot assume that the node serving as the leader/director will always be present. Decentralized distributed processing is important for distributed sensor networks, as well as V2X and military applications, because often times there is no clear "leader" and the computing cluster must be able to function with any node missing.

3.2   CLES Core Language Design

Despite their vastly dissimilar objectives and limiting factors, the use cases of vehicle platooning and military JDAC represent some of the most prevalent problems in the development of modern day embedded systems.

To satisfy the additional design drivers of programmability, flexibility, and interoperability, our CLES domain specific language features a limited but powerful set of verbs and a plain-text, JSON-formatted, response structure. The primary benefits to the RESTful architectural style is the ability to expose a limitless set of capabilities as nouns while constraining their interface semantics to a simple set of 5 verbs (Table 1).

CLES addresses the minimal latency and overhead requirements with a lightweight CLES service for point-to-point communication. With this solution, the computationally weaker nodes do not need to support a full CLES runtime, only a direct point-to-point interface, designed to integrate directly into a host application. CLES leverages this point-to-point service to solve the timeliness requirements as discussed in Sect. 3.4. This service has been designed and explored to solve the challenges present in the *Platooning* use case.

The design requirement of *decentralized* task management was tackled by designing and implementing a separate standalone runtime for CLES that allows for registration of tasks that can then be invoked remotely. Rather than integrating into an application like the point-to-point service, the CLES runtime is designed to be run as a standalone service, with a single runtime for each embedded device that supports remote task submissions. The runtime has been designed and discussed in future sections to solve the JDAC distributed processing problems while maintaining flexibility and interoperability with the point-to-point service.

Table 1. CLES verbs

Verb	Usage
Pull	Get Data Once
Push	Send Parameter and Data
Delegate	Send Parameter, Get Result
Bind	Register to Get Persistent Updates
Update	Send Update to Bound Users

3.3   CLES SDK Interface Definition

The CLES library interface for integrating with applications is simple but powerful. The interface constructs a *CLES_Service*, which requires a device name to expose externally and a network interface with the port to bind to. After constructing a service, each CLES verb has its own registration interface, whose *Register<Verb>Function* definitions bridge the application

$$\langle\text{CLES Command}\rangle \models \langle\text{verb}\rangle \langle\text{noun}\rangle \tag{1}$$

$$\langle\text{verb}\rangle \models pull \mid push \mid delegate \mid bind \mid update \tag{2}$$

$$\langle\text{noun}\rangle \models \langle\text{remote target}\rangle : \langle\text{task name}\rangle/\langle\text{task parameters}\rangle \tag{3}$$

$$\langle\text{remote target}\rangle \models \langle\text{generic string}\rangle \tag{4}$$

$$\langle\text{task name}\rangle \models \langle\text{generic string}\rangle \tag{5}$$

$$\langle\text{task parameters}\rangle \models \langle\text{parameter}\rangle \mid \langle\text{task parameters}\rangle\langle\text{parameter}\rangle \tag{6}$$

$$\langle\text{parameter}\rangle \models \langle\text{generic string}\rangle \tag{7}$$

$$\langle\text{generic string}\rangle \models [a - zA - Z0 - 9]+ \tag{8}$$

Fig. 2. CLES Backus-Naur Form (BNF) grammar

to the CLES external interface. For example, to expose the capability for other devices to retrieve this application's timestamp, the developer would first craft a function such as *CLES_Response getSystemTime()* which internally fills and returns a *CLES_Response* object with a key-value pair for system time. Next, the developer would associate this function with the verb PULL by calling *RegisterPullFunction"systemTime", getSystemTime)*. After registering all verbs and associated functions, the *CLES_Service* can be started with *run()* to accept external connections. Finally, a second device with its own CLES service could request the system time from the first device by calling *makeCLESRequest("PULL device1:systemTime")*. To pass parameters, such as timezone into *getSystemTime(vector<string>args)*, the CLES Request can be extended as per the DSL grammar (Fig. 2), with the example: *"PULL device1:systemTime/UTC"*.

To enable the *systemTime* capability at a device level, create a DELEGATE capability in the CLES runtime with a similar process substituding PULL for DELEGATE. The SDK compiles all application interfaces into a plugin that can be loaded by the CLES runtime rather than compiled into an application.

Listing 1.1. CLES Interface

```
CLES_Service(deviceName, interface, port);
bool register<Verb>Function(name, function);
void run();
void stop();
CLES_Response makeCLESRequest(CLES_Request);
```

3.4   CLES Point-to-Point Service

The CLES Point-to-Point service reduces the number of additional data transmissions and translations (hops) from source to destination. This design facet also makes it unnecessary for all CLES users to support the full runtime. Henceforth, we refer to "Point-to-Point" as "P2P," which is not to be confused with "Peer-to-Peer.". The P2P CLES service closely mirrors the semantics of the

Java "net.http" interface. Our goal is to flatten the learning curve for developers already familiar with the ubiquitous HTTP, so they can quickly transfer their knowledge to the domain of embedded systems. Like the "net.http" interface, the P2P service achieves minimal hops and overhead by integrating an in-line function call to the networking layer from the parent application.

3.5   CLES Runtime and Task Distribution

The CLES runtime introduces novel asymmetric task registration and remote access to meet the unique execution constraints of its target domain. The CLES runtime is designed around the concept of "a distributed collection of thread-pools." In this design, each device that processes externally-provided tasks must have a standalone CLES runtime service, similar to the service of the worker nodes in container orchestration architectures. One key difference between CLES and Container Orchestration solutions is that every machine with a CLES runtime serves both as a *leader* and *worker* node. In this way, each node can process tasks passed to it from an external source with the DELEGATE verb, as well as pass commands to other nodes. Internally, each runtime comprises a thread-pool that processes all received commands. This can be extended to support task sharing and stealing, much like a modern threadpool. The established distributed synchronization properties of a threadpool ensure mutual exclusion, thus preventing all deadlocks, livelocks, and task duplication.

Another difference between CLES and Container Orchestration is how capabilities are added to a node. Instead of dynamically deploying containers, incurring high bandwidth costs, each CLES runtime locally registers plugins at startup. The asymmetric nature of device-specific plugins and leaderless coordination support the flexibility and timeliness requirements in highly heterogeneous embedded environments.

While the CLES runtime supports all of the previously mentioned verbs, it uniquely supports processing of the DELEGATE verb. DELEGATE represents the CLES equivalent of adding a task to a threadpool, while the remaining verbs represent common actions of point-to-point communication. A notable usage of the runtime outside of DELEGATE paradigm is creating runtime plugins that expose PULL interfaces to data shared across all applications on a device, such as UTC time, processor load, or RAM usage.

3.6   CLES Implementation

Given OS and language limitations stemming from the *heterogeneous* requirement, we developed CLES in accordance with the C++17 standard, without third-party libraries. C++ remains an industry standard and the primary development language for both the defense and automotive industries.

To address the variety of network architectures and achieve interoperability, CLES supports native IP communication protocols UDP and TCP for its networking layer. IP is also universally accepted and nearly all modern networking protocols, i.e. WiFi, data link, Bluetooth, etc. support IP as a method of routing communication between devices. The CLES service wrapper abstracts this interface, which opens opportunity for future development to extend this interface to include memory mapped I/O and common data distribution platforms such as Google ProtoBuf, ActiveMQ, and DDS. Embedding the network interface into the CLES SDK interface caters to the desires of the embedded systems community because unlike solutions such as the RQL mobile device runtime [12], and data brokers like ActiveMQ, P2P CLES avoids passing of information between third-party runtimes or brokers. This helps reduce latency, but also supports deterministic real-time scheduling as defined by the parent application because this interface is called in-line directly by the parent with no additional non-deterministic processing constraints or data transmissions.

The Software Development kit (SDK) for CLES consists of a supporting static C++ library for extending an application with point-to-point service, the CLES runtime, and all necessary interfaces to create a plugin to extend the runtime capabilities. Plugins for the runtime follow the traditional C++ DLL interface, which is common across plugin architectures. A developer can create a plugin by using the provided CLES development SDK library, and exposing the required interfaces to the CLES runtime, which are as simple as defining an interface to the desired capability.

Currently, the automotive industry relies on real-time operating systems to host V2X applications, with the top competitors including QNX by blackberry, VxWorks by Wind River Systems, and the newer Real-Time Linux (RT-Linux) also by Wind River. This SDK has been compiled and run on both Windows and Linux based systems, which guarantees compatibility with QNX and RT-Linux, and is theoretically able to port to VxWorks and other Operating Systems with minimal modification to system calls for IP for network interface configuration and socket control.

4   Evaluation

We evaluated CLES via micro-benchmarks, a representative application of Distributed Stochastic Gradient Descent, and design case studies. The benchmarks isolate the performance characteristics of relevant parameters; the application implementation of Distributed Stochastic Gradient Descent validates CLES usability and flexibility for distributed workloads; the case studies demonstrate the applicability of CLES in meeting the tight timing requirements of vehicle platooning and the flexibility requirements of task allocations with U.S. Military Joint All Domain Command and Control. Our evaluation is driven by the following questions: (1) Does CLES meet the timeliness requirements for vehicle platooning? (2) Is the plain-text packet structure of CLES compatible with the network protocols of distributed embedded systems? (3) How does the developer workload of CLES compare to that of traditional programming models? Given that CLES consists of both a Point-to-Point service and task allocation runtime, each was evaluated against different criteria.

4.1 P2P CLES Performance and Micro-Benchmarks

CLES has been designed to prioritize programmability while maintaining timeliness constraints. To capture the performance of the CLES P2P service, we evaluated the round trip time overhead, packet size, and implementation source lines of code. This process was also completed for the traditional method of constructing a serialized packet with an ICD definition and implementing a minimal TCP client-server connection.

Both methods were tested with the task of having a client request a localization packet from a server analogous to basic V2V requirements. The CLES verb PULL was used to capture both the overhead of a server parsing a CLES message and constructing a JSON object with the response. PULL represents the worst case overhead because it exercises both a send and receive using all basic CLES functions that add overhead. Additionally, both the ICD and CLES implementation use TCP as their network protocol. Benchmarking was conducted both locally on a single machine, and across a WiFi network to isolate the CLES overhead in the total Round-Trip-Time (RTT). The localization packet contained a timestamp, latitude, longitude, forward velocity, and forward acceleration (Fig. 3).

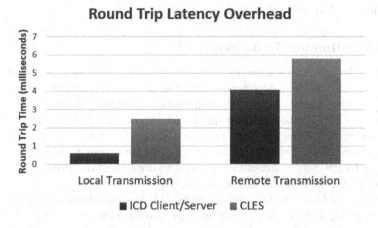

Fig. 3. CLES Latency Micro-benchmark

Each category of analysis has an important takeaway. First, the total latency overhead for a CLES PULL versus a traditional ICD packet is around 1.5 ms. When considering the CLES verb paring BIND and UPDATE, continuous updates remove half of the round trip time, and as such, this additional overhead is within 10% of the total allowable 100 ms latency for vehicle platooning [2]. Another factor to consider with total latency overhead is scaling. The recursive descent parser used within the language definition for CLES, while theoretically achieving a maximum performance scaling of $O(n)$, is reduced to a constant time $O(1)$ performance because the scaling factor is based on the size of the CLES request itself, which is limited to a single verb and noun pair with additional adverbs being passed directly to a registered function. On the receiving end of the function, parsing a JSON object is bound by a complexity of $O(n)$ relative to the size of the message, which in most cases, like with localization, remains constant to constrain the parse to a realistic operational complexity of $O(1)$. Given that the request and response are handled directly in-line with the parent application, and both ends reduce to a given constant time complexity $O(1)$, this experimental result of 1.5 ms additional overhead is directly transferable across all CLES interfaces with only minimal differences in the target behavior from processor frequency and JSON response size.

Second, the packet size overhead, while being larger by a factor of three (132 bytes for CLES), is still a small fraction of the 65,535 byte maximum allowable transmission size for TCP or UDP. The CLES JSON Response is also well within the single transmission frame size of 1500 bytes for 5G [3] which indicates that no additional overhead will be required to transmit the larger JSON packet. Finally, the implementation of CLES requires 30 lines of code, which represents 1/10th as many lines of code as the traditional ICD method with a TCP client and server. Equally as important as lines of code are the complexity and programmability. Implementing the CLES solution required no knowledge of the TCP/IP stack and sockets, thus significantly reducing the learning curve for extending networked capabilities within an application.

4.2   CLES Runtime Evaluation

The CLES Runtime is designed to provide flexibility and programmability for distributing processing tasks across multiple devices. To evaluate these criteria, the CLES Runtime was used to implement Distributed Stochastic Gradient Descent (D-SGD) to demonstrate that it can be effectively distributed with CLES, achieving satisfactory performance. Because Stochastic Gradient Descent is a fundamental mathematical principle of machine learning, this use case confirms that CLES can be successfully applied to implement distributed processing solutions in this and similar domains (Fig. 4).

The Parallel Gradient Descent algorithm [13] was distributed using the Sandblaster Limited-Memory Broyden-Fletchger-Goldfarb-Shanno (L-BFGS) model [5]. This model divides the data set into batches called data shards that are processed in parallel using a central management node to coordinate their distribution and subsequent consolidation.

Two machines, a workstation PC and a laptop, each hosted a CLES runtime with a plugin for single-threaded stochastic gradient descent on a supplied data shard. The data set was loaded on each machine to remove the additional overhead of data transfer, thus isolating the performance impact of CLES. The management node divided up the data set into data shards, represented as parameters for data set access, and used CLES to DELEGATE the processing of those shards to the CLES runtimes.

The data set used to demonstrate the D-SGD was a 2-Dimensional, 2 class linear classification problem with 100,000 normally distributed data points per

---

Algorithm 1 SGD($\{c^1, \ldots, c^m\}, T, \eta, w_0$)

---
for $t = 1$ **to** T **do**
   Draw $j \in \{1 \ldots m\}$ uniformly at random.
   $w_t \leftarrow w_{t-1} - \eta \partial_w c^j(w_{t-1})$.
end for
return w_T.

Algorithm 2 ParallelSGD($\{c^1, \ldots c^m\}, T, \eta, w_0, k$)

---
for all $i \in \{1, \ldots k\}$ **parallel do**
   $v_i = \text{SGD}(\{c^1, \ldots c^m\}, T, \eta, w_0)$ on client
end for
Aggregate from all computers $v = \frac{1}{k} \sum_{i=1}^{k} v_i$ and **return** v

---

Fig. 4. Parallel Stochastic Gradient Descent [13]

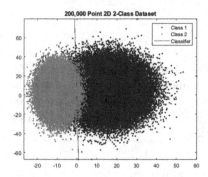

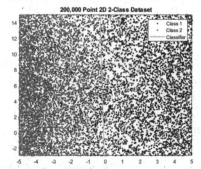

Fig. 5. Data set with classifier   **Fig. 6.** Zoomed data set with classifier

class (Fig. 5). To evaluate the additional overhead of CLES, the dataset was classified both individually on the laptop and the PC using a single thread, and four threads. These results were then compared to equivalent tests using the CLES tuntime and management node to control the distribution of tasks using CLES DELEGATE (Fig. 6).

The D-SGD results in Table 2 validate a design pattern common to Sandblaster L-BFGS and other data processing distribution methods of minimizing communication necessary to coordinate nodes. In the D-SGD workload, relatively few messages with a low total overhead are used to coordinate large processing workloads. The minimal cost of CLES is demonstrated as 10 ms locally in the comparison of running four threads on the PC, and DELEGATING 4 data shards to the PC CLES runtime from a manager on the same machine using CLES. The overhead, less than 0.5% of the total processing time, is a minimal cost for allowing distribution beyond a single machine. The difference between managing CLES D-SGD locally from the PC (2190 ms) and remotely (2290 ms) represents the additional network overhead of 100 ms. This highlights the CLES performance impact as minimal compared to overall network performance.

The previously demonstrated minimal overhead of coordination relative to absolute data processing time emphasizes the design priority of flexibility

Table 2. D-SGD performance results

Local Multi-Threaded D-SGD		
Test	Average Execution Time (ms)	Mean-Squared Error
1 Thread PC	8150	0.0198995
1 Thread Laptop	9360	0.0198995
4 Threads PC	2180	0.0198977
4 Threads Laptop	2500	0.0198977
CLES DELEGATE D-SGD		
4 PC Threads, PC Request	2190	0.0198977
4 PC Threads, Laptop Request	2290	0.0198977
8 Threads Both Machines, Laptop Request	2150	0.0198978

and programmability for distributed workloads. The CLES implementation for extending SGD into a plugin and creating a management node to make the DELEGATE requests and combine responses requires less than 300 source lines of C++. This implementation could be similarly adapted to any distribution domain with similar manager-worker semantics.

Platooning CLES Solution. CLES fits the design requirements: it is quick to implement, compatible with real-time OSs, reliant on IP networking, reducing latency via a Point-to-Point service, while its RESTful DSL request and response structure supports quick upgradability, backwards compatibility, and inter-manufacturer operability. Optionally, a C++ vehicle control module allows for directly including CLES to meet real-time deterministic timing constraints.

After establishing CLES as a viable middleware solution the integration with CLES was designed. As discussed above, we selected the Point-to-Point service, as dynamic task allocation is out of scope, while minimal hops with deterministic behavior was desired. The minimal request and response structure is for each vehicle to request persistent updates of localization data from the vehicle directly in front of it, and the platoon leader [10]. The design requirement of persistent updates naturally fits with the CLES verb pairing BIND and UPDATE. A CLES BIND request for localization messages from all vehicles on the local network created by 802.11p or 5G covers all required functionality. Finally, to fulfill this BIND, each vehicle would post an UPDATE of their localization, which would be sent to all bound vehicles in the local network.

JDAC CLES Solution. The OS flexibility, integration with the OSI IP stack, and ease of development of CLES make it a suitable solution for implementing Joint All-Domain Command and Control (JDAC).

In this scenario, given the core design requirement of task allocation, such as requesting a processing task from the satellite, and a strike task from the strike assets, the CLES runtime was explored as a solution. First, the satellite exposes its ability to process FMV into *Tracks* by integrating the CLES runtime and creating a plugin for the DELEGATE capability *FMV_Processing*. This capability accepts required metadata to begin receiving FMV and returns the calculated *Track*. Second, the reconnaissance aircraft integrates the CLES runtime with its Operational Flight Program (OFP). The OFP of the aircraft upon collecting FMV uses the CLES runtime to DELEGATE remote processing to any asset with the *FMV_Processing* capability. The aircraft OFP after receiving the *CLES_Resonse* with a *Track*, leverages the CLES P2P service and the POST verb to send the track to all other bound parties. The mission center with a CLES P2P service, BINDS to the *Tracks* from the reconnaissance aircraft. The data is then presented to humans in the loop to make critical strike decisions. After a strike decision, the command station then sends a DELEGATE strike task to an available asset that registered a compatible strike capability such as the fighter aircraft.

5 Conclusion

Modern embedded systems—autonomous vehicle-to-vehicle communication, smart cities, and military Joint All-Domain Operations—feature increasingly heterogeneous distributed components. Existing embedded system solutions for communication and networking are inflexible, tightly coupled to wireless protocols, and expensive to develop to satisfy the requirements. On the other extreme, modern software solutions for distributing data, allocating dynamic tasks, and deploying applications cannot satisfy embedded system requirements because of centralized management, operating system constraints, and heavyweight middleware.

This paper has presented a Representational State Transfer (REST) architecture, designed and implemented to uniquely complement the constraints of embedded systems development, such as language, operating system, latency, and networking protocols. Our solution features a domain-specific language, called the Communication Language for Embedded Systems (CLES), that supports both traditional point-to-point data communication and allocation of decentralized distributed tasks. We demonstrated how CLES can increase programmability and flexibility of developing communication in embedded systems with marginal performance impacts through representative micro-benchmarks, a distributed stochastic gradient descent use case, and application case studies.

Acknowledgements. The authors thank the anonymous reviewers, whose insightful comments helped improve this paper. NSF supported this research through the grant #1717065.

References

1. Boban, M., Kousaridas, A., Manolakis, K., Eichinger, J., Xu, W.: Connected roads of the future: use cases, requirements, and design considerations for vehicle-to-everything communications. IEEE Veh. Technol. Mag. **13**(3), 110–123 (2018). https://doi.org/10.1109/MVT.2017.2777259
2. Campolo, C., Molinaro, A., Araniti, G., Berthet, A.O.: Better platooning control toward autonomous driving: an LTE device-to-device communications strategy that meets ultralow latency requirements. IEEE Veh. Technol. Mag. **12**(1), 30–38 (2017). https://doi.org/10.1109/MVT.2016.2632418
3. Cominardi, L., Contreras, L.M., Bcrnardos, C.J., Berberana, I.: Understanding QoS applicability in 5G transport networks. In: 2018 IEEE International Symposium on Broadband Multimedia Systems and Broadcasting (BMSB), pp. 1–5. IEEE (2018). https://doi.org/10.1109/BMSB.2018.8436847. https://ieeexplore.ieee.org/document/8436847/
4. Congressional Research Service: Joint all-domain command and control (jadc2) (2020). https://fas.org/sgp/crs/natsec/IF11493.pdf
5. Dean, J., et al.: Large scale distributed deep networks. In: Pereira, F., Burges, C.J.C., Bottou, L., Weinberger, K.Q. (eds.) Advances in Neural Information Processing Systems, vol. 25. Curran Associates, Inc. (2012). https://proceedings.neurips.cc/paper/2012/file/6aca97005c68f1206823815f66102863-Paper.pdf
6. Fielding, R.T.: Architectural styles and the design of network-based software architectures, vol. 7. University of California, Irvine, Irvine (2000)
7. Force, U.A.: U-2 federal lab achieves flight with kubernetes. https://www.af.mil/News/Article-Display/Article/2375297/u-2-federal-lab-achieves-flight-with-kubernetes/
8. Martínez, I.S.H., Salcedo, I.P.O.J., Daza, I.B.S.R.: IoT application of WSN on 5G infrastructure. In: 2017 International Symposium on Networks, Computers and Communications (ISNCC), pp. 1–6 (2017). https://doi.org/10.1109/ISNCC.2017.8071989
9. S. Arefizadeh, A.T., Zelenko, I.: Platooning in the presence of a speed drop: a generalized control model (2017). http://arxiv.org/abs/1709.10083
10. Swaroop, D., Hedrick, J.K.: Constant spacing strategies for platooning in automated highway systems. J. Dyn. Syst. Measur. Control **121**(3), 462 (1999)
11. Yang, L., Dihua, S., Fei, X., Jian, Z.: Study of autonomous platoon vehicle longitudinal modeling. In: IET International Conference on Intelligent and Connected Vehicles (ICV 2016) (2016)
12. Song, Z., Chadha, S., Byalik, A., Tilevich, E.: Programming support for sharing resources across heterogeneous mobile devices. In: Proceedings of the 5th International Conference on Mobile Software Engineering and Systems - MOBILESoft '18, pp. 105–116 (2018)
13. Zinkevich, M., Weimer, M., Li, L., Smola, A.: Parallelized stochastic gradient descent. In: Lafferty, J., Williams, C., Shawe-Taylor, J., Zemel, R., Culotta, A. (eds.) Advances in Neural Information Processing Systems, vol. 23. Curran Associates, Inc. (2010). https://proceedings.neurips.cc/paper/2010/file/abea47ba24142ed16b7d8fbf2c740e0d-Paper.pdf

When Neural Networks Using Different Sensors Create Similar Features

Hugues Moreau[1,2](✉) [iD], Andréa Vassilev[1], and Liming Chen[2] [iD]

[1] Université Grenoble Alpes, CEA, Leti, 38000 Grenoble, France
{hugues.moreau,andrea.vassilev}@cea.fr
[2] Department of Mathematics and Computer Science, Ecole Centrale de Lyon,
University of Lyon, Ecully, France
{hugues.moreau,liming.chen}@ec-lyon.fr

Abstract. Multimodal problems are omnipresent in the real world: autonomous driving, robotic grasping, scene understanding, etc... Instead of proposing to improve an existing method or algorithm: we will use existing statistical methods to understand the features in already-existing neural networks. More precisely, we demonstrate that a fusion method relying on Canonical Correlation Analysis on features extracted from Deep Neural Networks using different sensors is equivalent to looking at the output of the networks themselves.

Keywords: Multimodal sensors · Deep learning · Transport Mode detection · Inertial sensors · Canonical Correlation Analysis

1 Introduction

Picture a rural scenery: in the countryside, the wind blows through a batch of trees. One can imagine hearing the sound of the wind in the leaves, seeing the branches bend to the gusts of wind, or even feeling the cold air on their skin. All of these stimuli are linked to a single event. Our world is multi-modal: at all times, any event can be captured using a broad diversity of channels. Many real-life problems rely on using multiple modalities: vision and LIDAR sensors for autonomous driving, visual and haptic feedback for robotic grasping, humans even use multiple modalities to understand each other, reading on the lips of their interlocutors.

In the Machine Learning community, a great deal of literature exists to leverage multiple sensors. Some publications use problem-specific solutions, but some approaches are generic: one can, for instance, give the information from all sensors to a single neural network. Or, one can choose to create one network per sensor, to train them to solve the problem the best they can, and to merge the predictions afterwards. In particular, Ahmad *et al.* and Imran *et al.* ([2,5] respectively) performed the fusion using a statistical tool named Canonical Correlation Analysis (CCA), in order to find correlations within two sets of features

S. Deng et al. (Eds.): MobiCASE 2021, LNICST 434, pp. 69–82, 2022.
https://doi.org/10.1007/978-3-030-99203-3_5

produced by neural networks trained separately. Their goal was to create a new common representation from all sensors for a gesture recognition problem.

The CCA operation has been used in multiple publications to understand deep neural networks working on a single-modality problem, [8,11,12]. In particular, Roeder *et al.* [13] demonstrated that several architectures, using the same input data, are approximately equal up to a linear transformation. This impressive result was soon followed by McNeely-White *et al.* [10], who showed a similar result for networks working on face recognition.

The present work extends this claim and helps to understand the similarity between the feature neural networks learnt from different sensors. More precisely, we show that the most correlated components between the features from different *sensors* are equal to the class components, *i.e.*, the vectors forming the column of the weight matrix from the classification layer. The most short-term consequence is that the fusion method introduced in [2,5] is equivalent to an average of predictions. To sum up, our contributions are the following:

- we demonstrate that the CCA recomputes the information from the classification layer of the network
- we apply this reasoning to show the fusion methods introduced in [2,5] is identical to a mere average of class logits.

We want to emphasize that we use existing methods and algorithms to reach a new conclusion, which is to show that the use of CCA for data fusion can be replaced by a much less complex equivalent. The rest of this work is organized as follows: Sect. 2 introduces some notations, reviews the Canonical Correlation Analysis, and explains some fundamental concepts to understand our work. Then, we show how the present work is novel compared to the rest of the literature in Sect. 3. Finally, Sect. 4 explains the experiments we led and analyzes the results.

2   Problem Position

2.1   Deep Feature Extraction

Let us consider two networks, either two initializations of networks using the same sensor, or networks using different sensors. The most common way to extract features from a network is to record the hidden features right before the last layer (the classification layer), as Fig. 1 illustrates. We name these feature matrices X_1 and X_2. An important point to note is that these features are computed from the same samples: if the ith line of X_1 is recorded using an accelerometer segment recorded at a given date, the ith line of X_2 must be computed from data (for instance, magnetometer data) recorded at the same exact moment as the accelerometer segment. The sensors may differ, but the intrinsic samples (and their order in the feature matrices $X_{1,2}$) must correspond.

We call $W_i \in \mathbb{R}^{n_c \times n_i}$ (where n_c is the number of classes and n_i is the number of features from each feature matrix) the *class components*, that is, the column

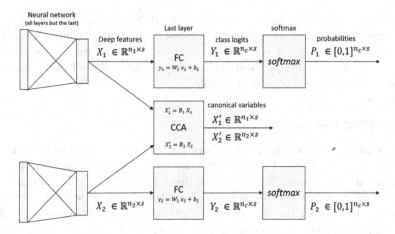

Fig. 1. The extraction of deep features. n_c is the number of classes, n_i is the number of features from each feature matrix, and s is the number of samples

vectors of the weights of the last fully-connected layer (the middle layer in Fig. 1). As with every other matrix multiplication, one can understand the classification process $x \to W_i.x$ (we omit the bias) as a series of scalar products with the n_c column vectors of W_i: for each class c, the scalar product between each feature vector x and the cth column of W_i gives the logit of class c, a real number giving the likelihood for the sample to belong in class c (the higher the number, the higher the chances that the sample belongs in the class). These logits are then fed into the softmax operation, in order to obtain a series of probabilities (n_c numbers between 0 and 1 that sum to 1).

2.2 Canonical Correlation Analysis

Canonical Correlation Analysis is a statistical tool that takes two feature matrices X_1, X_2, and returns a series of linear combinations of each of these features $X'1 = B_1.X_1$, $X'_2 = B_2.X_2$ (where B_1, B_2 are basis change matrices). These new features are defined recursively: the first column of X'_1 and the first column of X'_2 (the first *canonical variables*) are computed such that the correlation between them is maximized. Then, the second columns of these matrices maximize the correlation between each other while being decorrelated to the previously computed (the correlation between the first and the second columns of X'_1 is zero). The subsequent columns are constructed the same way, by maximising the mutual correlation between matrices X'_1 and X'_2, while being decorrelated to previously computed components. Note that this requires the matrices X_i to be full-rank so that we have enough components. In practice, we use PCA to obtain full-rank feature matrices (we remove the components that account for less than 0.01 % of the cumulative variance).

Similarly to the class components, the *canonical components* are the column vectors of the B_i, and we will compare the first of them to the class components.

There are as many canonical components as there are input features in the feature matrix $X_{1,2}$, but we are only interested in the *first* n_c components. They correspond to the n_c *most* correlated components one can find in the features. We want to show there is a linear relationship between these first n_c canonical components and the n_c class components.

2.3   A Simplistic Example

Let us consider an unrealistic, but illustrative, example, and let us imagine that the class logits were equal across networks $Y_1 = Y_2$. One should notice that the logits are linear combinations of features $Y_i = W_i.X_i$[1]. This means that one can find linear combinations of features that correlate perfectly with each other. Yet, because of the way the canonical components are computed, these class components will always appear first among the canonical components. In practice, the logits are not equal, but they only need to be correlated enough to each other.

Once this is understood, it is easier to understand the main claim of this work. If we consider two networks, producing the sets of features X_1 and X_2, that succeed fairly at the same classification task, then, the logits Y_1 and Y_2 produced by those networks will be correlated. The last layer of the networks is linear, in other words, the class components can be found among both feature vectors X_1 and X_2 with a simple linear transformation ($Y_i = W_i.X_i$). This means that if one applies CCA to the couple of feature matrices (X_1, X_2), one can find the class components W_i among the first components of B_i.

In particular, this means computing the sum of the canonical variables ($X_1' + X_2'$, as [2,5] do) is equivalent to summing the logits $Y_1 + Y_2$. Figure 2 illustrates how the equality of the canonical components and the class components make the CCA fusion equivalent to a sum of the logits.

2.4   Extensions

Section 4.2 will detail the experiments we lead to demonstrate the correspondence between CCA components and classification components, both in the case of networks using the same sensor, and in the case of networks using different sensors.

One might wonder what are the causes of the phenomenon. If we sum up the previous sections, for CCA to pick up the class components, two conditions must be verified:

- The class logits of two networks must be more correlated than any other component of the feature space.

---

[1] In the following sections, we will omit the bias in the equation $Y_i = W_i.X_i + b_i$. As the CCA assumes that $X_{1,2}$ have zero mean, a necessary step prior to the computation of the canonical components is to remove the mean of the features X_i. This is why adding the constant bias b_i does not change anything to the reasoning.

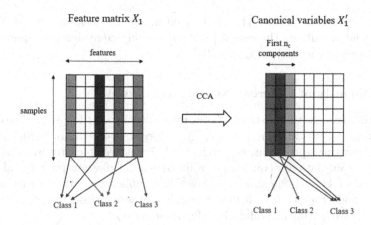

Fig. 2. The principle of the equality between class components and the first canonical components on a three-class problem. The colours in the different feature matrices denote the different information about the three classes. The feature vectors will undergo a matrix multiplication (denoted by the arrows under the left matrix); and the rows of the matrix the features are multiplied by are the class components. (Color figure online)

- We must apply CCA on the features from the last layer (so that there is a linear relationship between the features and the class logits).

The first condition seems to be verified in practice. For instance, [9] studied the prediction similarity of networks working on the same problem, and found that they are much more similar to each other than what their accuracies could lead to believe. As for the second condition, some publications work with CCA in other layers than the last [11,12] to explore the behaviour of neural networks. However, the verification of this second condition (especially finding an equivalent to the classification components in the earlier layers), is out of scope for this work.

3   Related Works

3.1   CCA as a Fusion Method

Two works [2,5] used the Canonical Correlation in a multimodal setting: in a problem with several sensors (each of them being able to bring some information about the problem), they both considered the following process: first, they trained one neural network per sensor. Then, they extracted the hidden representations from the last layer of each network. They computed the canonical variables (X_1' and X_2' with the notations from the previous section), then summed these components ($X_1' + X_2'$), before using a Machine Learning algorithm (SVM or KELM) to guess the final prediction from the result of the addition.

Table 7 from [5] shows the results are not very different from averaging of the output *probabilities* of each network. One of our contributions is to show that the CCA operation isolated the class logits in the first components of X_1' and X_2' and that classifying the sum $X_1' + X_2'$ is roughly equivalent to summing the output *logits* of each network, class by class.

3.2   Similarity of Different Neural Networks

The similarity between two neural networks is a well-studied subject. The closest publications to our work are the ones from Roeder *et al.* [13]. In 2020, they discovered that the representations learnt by different architectures working using the same input data are equal up to a linear transformation; for a broad diversity of tasks including classification. Since this publication, other works, such as [10], expanded the claim to a broad diversity of monomodal architectures and brought new experiments validating this information.

To uncover the similarity between deep models, others looked more at the predictions of networks. For instance, [3] studied the order in which different models learn to classify each sample, while [9] demonstrated that two neural networks classify the samples the same way.

However, all these studies work on monomodal problems, that is, problems with a single input (in most cases, image classification). In the other hand, we provide an example of the similarity between representations learnt with the same architectures, using different *sensors*. The implications are important: this means the networks learnt to exploit the information that remains common between sensors.

3.3   SVCCA and Improvements

Several publications worked to improve the computation of the similarity between two bases of features. The first one is SVCCA [12], a famous publication that popularized the use of CCA to measure the similarity between two networks. The idea is to use PCA (Singular Vector decomposition, hence the SV in the abbreviation) on each of the feature matrices to remove low-variance components (which are assumed to be noise), before applying CCA on the reduced feature matrices. We too apply PCA, but only to remove the components with negligible variance (we keep 99.99% of the variance). That is, we keep the 'noisy' low-variance components. To compare, the authors from [12] keep only 99% of the variance, that is, they remove 100 times more variance than us. This means the results we draw are more robust. Morcos *et al.* [11] also noticed the components found by the classic CCA could be noisy. When measuring the proximity between two sets of features X_1 and X_2, they still compute the CCA components $X_{1,2}'$, but instead of using the average of the correlations between X_1' and X_2', they choose one of the feature sets (let us say, X_1), and weight the correlation proportionally to the variance which is kept by each CCA component (*i. e.*, the variance of each component of X_1' divided by the total variance of X_1). This method, named Projection-Weighted CCA (PWCCA), is better at rejecting noise than SVCCA.

Finally, Kornblith *et al.* [8] extended upon this approach, by dividing the correlation by the relative variance of both bases (X_1' and X_2'). They named their method CKA (Centered Kernel Alignment) because they use the kernel trick to find better alignments than mere linear combinations.

As [8] states, these two methods are closely related. PWCCA [11] consists in re-weighting the CCA components by the variance of one base, while linear CKA consists in re-weighing the components by using both variances (relatively to the variance of the original sets $X_{1,2}$). To summarize, one can see PWCCA and CKA as different mixtures between PCA and CCA. One could wonder if the conclusions we drew here also apply in the case of PWCCA and CKA. We argue that this is the case, for the following reason: Kamoi *et al.* [7] showed that when a network deals with inliers (non-outliers), the components with the highest variance among the features are approximately equal to a combination of the class logits. This explains the high results of the 'PCA' curve in Sect. 4.2. We showed that the most correlated components are very similar to logits. As a consequence, we expect re-weighting the importance of the CCA components by the amount of variance accounted for by each component to enforce even further the proximity between class logits and most important components. However, this paper focuses on regular CCA, which means that the experiments extending our conclusions to kernel-CCA or CKA are out of scope.

4   Experiments

In this section, we will first reproduce the results from [12], in order to illustrate our experimental protocol (Sect. 4.2). Then, we will repeat this experiment mixing data from different sensors to show our main claim in Sect. 4.2.

4.1   Datasets

CIFAR10. We use the famous ResNet-56 network [4] on the CIFAR-10 Dataset. This is a Computer Vision classification problem, where the model has to classify low-resolution (32×32) images into ten classes. The dataset contains 50,000 training samples and 10,000 validation samples. We trained the network hyperparameters and architecture as the original publication [4] thanks to the code from [1].

The dataset has only one sensor (the RGB images), but we work with different initializations of networks that use the same modality. We use this dataset to provide a comparison with the rest of the literature on CCA with deep features, as most works chose to include a ResNet trained on CIFAR-10 [8,11,12].

SHL 2018 Dataset. The Sussex-Huawei Locomotion 2018 dataset is a Transport Mode detection problem. Organizers asked three participants to record the sensor values from several smartphones while travelling using different modes (walking, running, driving, *etc.*). Then, the data is published, and a yearly challenge is organized to get a precise evaluation of the state of the art. The 2018

Table 1. An overview of the SHL 2018 dataset

Sensors	Accelerometer, Gravity, Linear Acceleration, Gyrometer, Magnetometer, Orientation quaternion, barometric Pressure
Classes	Still, Walk, Run, Bike, Car, Bus, Train, Subway
Segment duration	60 s
Sampling frequency	100 Hz
Training samples	13,000
Validation samples	3,310

dataset is the first version of the challenge: only the data from a single user and a single smartphone (the one in the hand) is available for classification. The organizers released 16,310 annotated samples for training and validation (Table 1).

The dataset includes seven sensors (accelerometer, gravity, linear acceleration, gyrometer, magnetometer, orientation vector, barometric pressure), most of them having several axes (x, y, z). We will study three signals among them: the y axis of the gyrometer (Gyr_y), the norm of the acceleration (Acc_norm, as in [6]), and the norm of the magnetometer (Mag_norm). The accelerometer and gyrometer encode similar information (they record the inertial dynamics of the sensor) and are most useful when detecting walk, run, or bike segments. On the other hand, the norm of the magnetometer mostly changes when the sensor is close to a strong magnetic field: far from any ferromagnetic object, its values stays close to $40\,\mu$T (the value of the Earth's magnetic field). But this sensor can go up to $200\,\mu$T when a strong magnetic field is present (for instance, when the sensor is close to a ferromagnetic object or even an electrical engine). This is why we think this sensor will be best to detect the train or subway classes from the rest. To summarize, the accelerometer and gyrometer are expected to be similar to each other, while these sensors encode different information than the magnetometer. This is intended to represent different relatedness between sensors.

We use the same approach as in [6], each signal is first converted into a two-dimensional spectrogram (a time-frequency diagram) using short term Fourier transform. The frequency axis of the spectrogram is rescaled using a logarithmic scale, in order to give more resolution to the lower frequencies. This method aims to give better resolution to the 2–3 Hz frequency bands (which are the most useful to distinguish the Walk, Run, and Bike segments), while still keeping the highest frequencies available. See [6] for more information and illustrations. For each sensor, we obtain a $48 \times 48 \times 1$ spectrogram, that is fed into a CNN which architecture is simple: three convolutional layers (with 16, 32, and 64 filters), and two fully-connected layers (with 128 hidden features and 8 output features). See [6] for details about hyperparameter or training process.

To illustrate, on three random initializations, the average validation F1-score of each of these individual sensors is 89% for the accelerometer, 80 % for the gyrometer, and 67 % for the magnetometer.

In both experiments, we will use a train set to train the models, extract the features, compute the base change with CCA, and, when applicable, retrain the models. The validation sets only go through trained models and already-computed base changes, before being used to display a result. We want to emphasize that when dealing with multimodal sensors, each network was only trained on a single modality: the network using the accelerometer never saw the gyrometer or magnetometer data, and so on.

4.2 Studying Component Similarity with Subspace Projection

In this section, we will reproduce and extend the experiments from [12] (Fig. 2 from this work). As Fig. 3 illustrates, we start from a trained network, we extract the hidden features form the last layer, then we project on a subspace of inferior dimension, before re-injecting the features in the network to measure the performance. If the performance is intact, it means that the n_c class components are unaffected by the projection. In other words, it means the class components already belong in the image of the projection. In particular, when the dimension of the image of the projection is $n_s = n_c$, and if the performance is unchanged, it means that the n_c class components belong in the subspace spanned by the n_s most correlated components, which implies the existence of a linear relationship between the families (as the canonical components and class components are both linearly independent families of vectors).

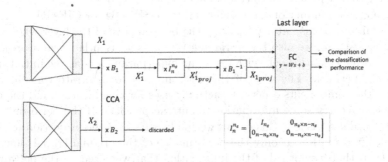

Fig. 3. The principle of the subspace projection experiment: $P_1 = B_1^{-1}.I_n^{n_s}.B_1$ projects X_1 onto a linear space with dimension n_s.

Note that when we use all features, we project on the original space, $i.e.$, we leave the data unchanged. The difference between the end of the curves (performance on pristine data) and the rest (altered data) will indicate the proximity between the considered subspace and class components.

The dimension and the way of choosing the subspace will vary: as in [12], we consider choosing the n most correlated components found with CCA (CCA_highest), the n features with the highest activation in absolute value (max_activation), and n features chosen randomly (random_selection). In order to provide comparisons, we add four reductions methods that are not included in [12]:

- *random orthogonal projection* (random_projection). Comparing the random selection of n components versus the projection on n components shows that the canonical basis does not play a particular role (*i.e.* selecting the values of n features is not particularly meaningful).
- *PCA*: Kamoi *et al.* [7] showed that the n_c components with the most variance are the components that will be used for classification. We project the features on the components with most variance to validate their findings.
- *least correlated components* (CCA_lowest): if the most correlated components are the class components, the components with lowest correlation should not include any relevant information for the problem.
- *CCA with random components* (CCA_random): one may argue that the CCA curve is above the others in [12] because CCA allows to create decorrelated components, which would mean that its components are less redundant than random directions. If this was the case, selecting random CCA components would be better than selecting components with a random projection.

To save time, we do not consider all the possible number of components: because we want a high resolution around n_c, we only considered the $2 * n_c$ first components (where n_c is the number of classes, 8 for SHL and 10 for CIFAR), and, after that, the number of components which are powers of 2 $(16, 32, ...)$, up to the maximal number of components (128 for SHL, 64 for CIFAR).

In addition to this, after measuring the performance of the layer when using projected features, we also try retraining the classification layer on a projected version of the validation set, with the same hyperparameters as the initial training of the network. The goal of this retraining is to illustrate the difference between the components a network actually uses for classification and the components that carry some information about the problem. If the performance of the retrained layer is low, this means we can be sure that the projection removed *all* useful information. If only the performance of the original layer is low, this only means that we got rid of the information that was used by the network.

Note that the CCA operation requires two databases. When we use CCA, we use a second matrix of features X_2, but only to compute X_1' (we discard X_2'). In the next section, this second network is another initialization of a network working with the same sensor, while the section after that shows experiments made with two networks using different sensors.

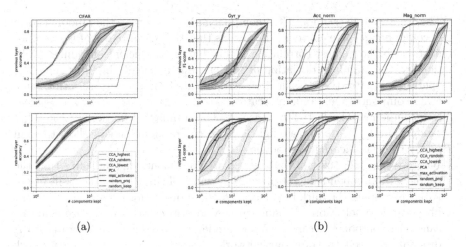

(a)   (b)

Fig. 4. The performance of the networks after projecting their features on subspaces with varying dimensions, on the CIFAR (a) and SHL (b) validation sets. The top row indicates the validation performance of the network as is, while the bottom row indicates the performance when retraining the classification layer on a projected training set. For each curve, the experiment was repeated 5 times, and the standard deviation is given by the width of the curve (which is sometimes too small to see). The dotted line highlights the performance with the n_c most correlated components. Best view in colour. (Color figure online)

Similarity Between Identical Sensors. Figure 4 shows the result of this experiment. We can draw several conclusions from it:

- The performance of the projection on the n_s highest variance components ('pca', green curve) is maximal for $n_s = n_c$: this verifies the findings of Kamoi *et al.* [7], the n_c components with highest variance are the class components.
- Similarly to Fig. 2 from [12], the most correlated components are more useful for the classification problem than a random choice of components from the canonical basis.
- The red curve (performance of the components with the highest correlation) is almost at its maximum for n_c components even before retraining, there is almost nothing to gain after n_c components. This validates our original claim these components correspond to the subspace used by the classification layer.
- The yellow curve (the components with lowest correlations), is under all the others. Before retraining, the performance of a projection on the n components with the lowest correlation is minimal, even when we select half the components. After retraining, the performance of these components is still well under the performance of random components: selecting the least correlated components effectively removed most of the classification information.

- The orange curve (random CCA components) is lower than the random choice of components (blue curves). This means that the performance of the components with the highest correlation is not due to an efficient encoding. Additionally, the standard deviation of this curve is unusually high: as the CCA operation isolates the classification components from the rest, selecting some of its components at random creates extremes situations: either a classification component is selected, or it is not. The standard deviations of the other random methods are not as high because the random choices allow to span partly the classification components.
- Before retraining, the two blue curves are equivalent, this indicates that the canonical components do not play any specific role in regards to classification. After retraining, the dark blue curve (random projection) is higher than light blue (random selection of canonical components). We hypothesize that the canonical components carry some redundancy between them because of the dropout we used to train our networks, and that re-training the network allows it to stop expecting this redundancy in the features it sees.

Similarity Between Two Different Sensors. We now lead experiments to verify our main contribution: the fact that the most correlated features are equal to classification components, even when the correlation is computed across sensors. This time, when computing CCA, we use features from a network using different sensors. In this section, we do not include any of the other dimensionality reduction methods (PCA, random projection and selection of components, maximal activation components) because those methods work with only one database: the results would be copies of the curves presented in Fig. 4.

Figure 5 shows that the performance is maximal when the number of components is close to 10 or 20, approximately. However, contrary to Fig. 4b, the performance is off by a few points when the number of selected components is equal to 8, the number of classes. This means that the equality between most correlated components and classification vectors is less strong than in the previous case when the CCA was computed from the same sensor. Still, the performance with only 8 components is high enough for us to conclude that the components computed with CCA overlap significantly with the classification components.

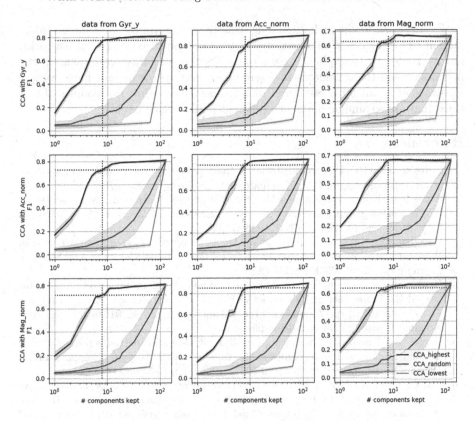

Fig. 5. The classification performance of classification layer using features projected on a subspace with varying dimension, when the CCA is computed thanks to data from another sensor. As in Fig. 4, one can see that the performance with the n_c most correlated components is close to the performance with all components. The graphs in the diagonal were generated using the same protocol as the first row of graphs in Fig. 4b. The dotted line highlights the performance with the n_c most correlated components. Best view in colour. (Color figure online)

5   Conclusion

We began by demonstrating the experiments from previous publications: the findings from Kamoi *et al.* [7], who showed that the components with most variance are the classification components, and Roeder *et al.* [13], who showed that CCA found the classification components when it is applied to features from monomodal networks using the same dataset. In a later section, we showed the same result held when applied to features learnt from different sensors, indicating that the networks exploit information that can be found across multiple sensors. The exact nature of this information, however, is yet to be found.

In addition to showing that the fusion method from [2,5] is unnecessarily complex, these results have strong implications for multimodal learning: in this situation, it may be unnecessary to add too many sensors, for neural networks would compute similar information.

Future work might include finding exactly the nature of the common information which is present in all sensors' signals and exploited by neural networks. Or, we could try to explain a paradox about the similarity we measured: the networks using the accelerometer, gyrometer, and magnetometer have average F1-scores of about 90%, 80%, and 67% (respectively). How can couples of features that are so similar have such different performance levels?

References

1. 2 ResNet_cifar10 - PyTorch Tutorial. https://pytorch-tutorial.readthedocs.io/en/latest/tutorial/chapter03_intermediate/3_2_2_cnn_resnet_cifar10/
2. Ahmad, Z., Khan, N.: Human action recognition using deep multilevel multimodal (M^2) fusion of depth and inertial sensors. IEEE Sens. J. **20**(3), 1445–1455 (2020). https://doi.org/10.1109/JSEN.2019.2947446
3. Hacohen, G., Choshen, L., Weinshall, D.: Let's agree to agree: neural networks share classification order on real datasets. In: International Conference on Machine Learning, pp. 3950–3960. PMLR (2020)
4. He, K., Zhang, X., Ren, S., Sun, J.: Deep residual learning for image recognition. In: 2016 IEEE Conference on Computer Vision and Pattern Recognition (CVPR), pp. 770–778 (2016). http://openaccess.thecvf.com/content_cvpr_2016/html/He_Deep_Residual_Learning_CVPR_2016_paper.html
5. Imran, J., Raman, B.: Evaluating fusion of RGB-D and inertial sensors for multimodal human action recognition. J. Ambient Intell. Human. Comput. **11**(1), 189–208 (2020). https://doi.org/10.1007/s12652-019-01239-9
6. Ito, C., Cao, X., Shuzo, M., Maeda, E.: Application of CNN for human activity recognition with FFT spectrogram of acceleration and gyro sensors. In: Proceedings of the 2018 ACM International Joint Conference and 2018 International Symposium on Pervasive and Ubiquitous Computing and Wearable Computers - UbiComp 2018, pp. 1503–1510. ACM Press, Singapore (2018). https://doi.org/10.1145/3267305.3267517, http://dl.acm.org/citation.cfm?doid=3267305.3267517
7. Kamoi, R., Kobayashi, K.: Why is the mahalanobis distance effective for anomaly detection? arXiv:2003.00402 [cs, stat], February 2020
8. Kornblith, S., Norouzi, M., Lee, H., Hinton, G.: Similarity of neural network representations revisited. In: International Conference on Machine Learning, pp. 3519–3529. PMLR, May 2019. http://proceedings.mlr.press/v97/kornblith19a.html
9. Mania, H., Miller, J., Schmidt, L., Hardt, M., Recht, B.: Model similarity mitigates test set overuse. In: Wallach, H., Larochelle, H., Beygelzimer, A., Alché-Buc, F.D., Fox, E., Garnett, R. (eds.) Advances in Neural Information Processing Systems, vol. 32. Curran Associates, Inc. (2019). https://proceedings.neurips.cc/paper/2019/file/48237d9f2dea8c74c2a72126cf63d933-Paper.pdf
10. McNeely-White, D., Sattelberg, B., Blanchard, N., Beveridge, R.: Exploring the interchangeability of CNN embedding spaces. arXiv:2010.02323 [cs], February 2021
11. Morcos, A., Raghu, M., Bengio, S.: Insights on representational similarity in neural networks with canonical correlation. Adv. Neural. Inf. Process. Syst. **31**, 5727–5736 (2018)
12. Raghu, M., Gilmer, J., Yosinski, J., Sohl-Dickstein, J.: SVCCA: singular vector canonical correlation analysis for deep learning dynamics and interpretability. In: Guyon, I., et al. (eds.) Advances in Neural Information Processing Systems, vol. 30, pp. 6076–6085. Curran Associates, Inc. (2017)
13. Roeder, G., Metz, L., Kingma, D.P.: On linear identifiability of learned representations. arXiv:2007.00810 [cs, stat], July 2020

Mobile Application with Data Analysis

Improving Togetherness Using Structural Entropy

Siyu Zhang[1], Jiamou Liu[3], Yiwei Liu[1], Zijian Zhang[2,3(✉)],
and Bakhadyr Khoussainov[4]

[1] School of Computer Science and Technology, Beijing Institute of Technology,
Beijing, China
{3120181073,yiweiliu}@bit.edu.cn
[2] School of Cyberspace Science and Technology, Beijing Institute of Technology,
Beijing, China
zhangzijian@bit.edu.cn
[3] School of Computer Science, The University of Auckland, Auckland, New Zealand
jiamou.liu@auckland.ac.nz
[4] School of Computer Science and Engineering,
University of Electronic Science and Technology of China, Chengdu, China
bmk@uestc.edu.cn

Abstract. A major theme in the study of social dynamics is the formation of a community structure on a social network, i.e., the network contains several densely connected region that are sparsely linked between each other. In this paper, we investigate the network integration process in which edges are added to dissolve the communities into a single unified network. In particular, we study the following problem which we refer to as togetherness improvement: given two communities in a network, iteratively establish new edges between the communities so that they appear as a single community in the network. Towards an effective strategy for this process, we employ tools from structural information theory. The aim here is to capture the inherent amount of structural information that is encoded in a community, thereby identifying the edge to establish which will maximize the information of the combined community. Based on this principle, we design an efficient algorithm that iteratively establish edges. Experimental results validate the effectiveness of our algorithm for network integration compared to existing benchmarks.

Keywords: Togetherness · Social network · Structural entropy

1 Introduction

1.1 Background

A social network consists of a set of individuals and their social bonds, forming a graph that exhibits a range of non-trivial statistical properties. *Community*

Z. Zhang—This paper is supported by National Natural Science Foundation of China No. 62172040, No. U1836212, No. 61872041.

structure amounts to one of the most prevalent properties of a social network. This property asserts that the graph can be broadly viewed as consisting of several densely-connected subgraphs, called *communities*, that are loosely connected between each other. Understanding the community structure provides key insights on the social compositional of the society. As social bonds can be seen as channels of interactions and passages of information and knowledge, communities are decisive in determining important social and behavioral traits such as social cohesion, self-identity, and the emergence of norms and trust [6,16,17].

A perpetual theme in studies on social networks is the dynamics of social ties. Countless scenarios exist where needs arise for updating the social bonds between individuals, thereby changing the graph structure. Many of these scenarios would involve intensions to integrate two communities into one. Take for example, business mergers and acquisitions which see two companies dissolve into a single entity, the marriage between two large families with complex relations, the assimilation process when immigrants arrive at a new country, and the healing process between two divided political fractions of a government. Creating a smooth unification between two disjoint communities in these scenarios is a common desirable outcome, which enhances the building of common grounds, mutual understanding, cooperation and conflict resolution.

The concept of *togetherness* [21] aims to capture the level of unity between two communities. This concept is defined in the context of *network integration*. In a nutshell, network integration corresponds to a process where communication channels are built, creating opportunities for interactions between individuals who otherwise belong to different communities. More formally, take a graph $G = (V, E)$ which represents a social network, i.e., V is the set of individuals and E is a set of (undirected) social ties. Suppose V is the union of several disjoint communities and C_1, C_2 are two of these communities. The network integration process adds a sequence of new edges $e_1, e_2, \ldots, e_\ell$ between nodes in C_1 and C_2 to form a graph G' in which members of $C_1 \cup C_2$ integrate into a single community. To be more precise, the authors of [21] introduced a number of methods to measure togetherness of two communities in an integrated network. These notions are based on the distances between nodes. In particular, the strongest notion among them is Δ-*togetherness*, which refers to the reciprocal of graph diameter in the integrated network. Several strategies were proposed in [20,21] to perform the network integration process to boost Δ-togetherness.

We argue that there is a need for another togetherness notion for network integration. Indeed, the *diameter* of a graph refers to the longest distance between any pair of nodes in the graph. Δ-togetherness assumes that the diameter of the integrated graph is the sole indicator for a united community. This is not accurate as there are situations where two communities are far from being fully integrated when the updated network reaches a small diameter (i.e., the diameter of the graph obtained in the "combined community" is no more than the diameters of any of the original communities). Consider, e.g., graph $G = (V, E)$ whose $V = \{v, u\} \cup U_1 \cup U_2$ where $U_1 = \{v_1, \ldots, v_n\}$ and $U_2 = \{u_1, \ldots, u_n\}$ where $n \in \mathbb{N}$, and E contains edges $\{v_i, v_j\}, \{u_i, u_j\}$ for any $i \neq j \in \{1, \ldots, n\}$ and

$\{v_i, u_j\}$ for any $i, j \in \{1, \ldots, n\}$ (thus U_1, U_2 forms a complete graph of size $2n$), and edges $\{v, v_i\}$, $\{u, u_i\}$ for any $i \in \{1, \ldots, n\}$. Now define two disjoint communities C_1, C_2 each of which has a graph structure that is isomorphic to G. To integrate these two communities, we add two new edge, the first between the copy of v in C_1 and the copy of v_1 in C_2, the second between the copy of u in C_2 and the copy of u_1 in C_1. Analyzing this graph it is apparent that $C_1 \cup C_2$ is far from being unified, despite achieving a good Δ-togetherness as:

1. Both the combined community (over $C_1 \cup C_2$) and the original communities (over C_1 and C_2, respectively) have diameter 3, suggesting high Δ-togetherness.
2. Each community C_i ($i \in \{1, 2\}$) has a *intra-density* (defined as the number of edges over nodes *within* the community) $(n(2n - 1) + 2n)/(2n + 2) = (2n^2 + n)/(2n + 2)$ which tends to ∞ as $n \to \infty$.
3. The communities C_1 and C_2 have a *inter-density* (defined as the number of edges over nodes *between* C_1 and C_2) $2/(4n + 4)$ which tends to 0 as $n \to \infty$.

To derive a more appropriate form of togetherness, it is necessary to recall our original motivation, namely, integrating two communities so that they eventually *appear* as a single community. The maturity of algorithms for *community detection* [12] means that one may assess togetherness through these algorithms. However, community detection algorithms vary vastly and can give inconsistent results. Going one step deeper, we look at what is behind the success of community detection algorithms, that is, they reveal regions of the graph that provide the most information regarding the network structure as a whole. The key to defining togetherness thus lies in revealing structural information of a graph.

1.2   Contributions

Motivated by the discussions above, we investigate network integration and togetherness in a graph that has a salient community structure. Our contribution include: (1) We invoke Li-Pan *structural information theory* [15] and borrow from their work the notion of *structural entropy* to quantify the amount of uncertainty within a graph. This notion allows us to determine how much information is gained through a community structure, which leads to our togetherness improvement problem. (2) We discover an interesting phenomenon, namely, *maximum degree principle* that link information gain through community structure with the degrees of nodes in the communities. Through this finding, we propose an efficient algorithm (TIE) for solving the togetherness improvement problem. (3) Finally, we demonstrate the effectiveness of our algorithm using experiments on both real-world and synthetic network datasets.

1.3   Related Work

Network Integration and Togetherness. Network integration was introduced as optimization problems by Moskvina and Liu in [19], who proposed two types of network integration problem: integrating a newcommer into a network (the so-called *network building* process), and combining two (sub-)networks into one through optimizing some global measure. Both of these problems involve adding a number of new edges to the graph iteratively and the objectives are to maximize certain notion of *social capital*, which refers to structure-based measurement of efficacies such as influence and cohesion [13,25]. In [19], the objectives are defined in terms of distances between nodes. Along the pathway of network building, [26,27] investigated building networks for a newcomer in a dynamic network, [7] added concerns to the cost of adding social ties, [24] generalized the objective from distance-based to other type of centrality measures, [8] further discussed the concept of social capital and proposed bonding and bridging social capital, and [28] focused on the situation where only partial observation is made by the newcomer.

While integrating a newcomer into a network mainly concerns social capital gained by the newcomer, the task of combining networks targets at global notions of social capital. In particular, *togetherness* embodies this type of social capital. There, Moskvina and Liu in [20] proposed a kind of network integration problem by establishing edges between two networks to minimize the diameter in the combined network. [21] proposed the notions of ∃-togetherness, ∀-togetherness, as well Δ-togetherness. They proposed the central-periphery (CtrPer) algorithm to facilitate the selection of new edges to be added to improve togetherness in the combined network.

We mention the two paradigms that persist in network science for quantifying properties of networks: The first is a *distance-based* approach which evaluates nodes based on the minimum number of hops, e.g., eccentricity and closeness centrality; the second is a *volume-based* approach which evaluates nodes based not only on distance but also on the number of paths connecting nodes [3]. Notions such as network flow and betweenness are all examples of tools within the latter paradigm. As discussed above, the togetherness notions introduced above are predominantly distance-based metrics, which is insufficient to correctly capture the community structure of a network. In this paper, we adopt a notion of structural entropy which is inherently a volume-based property.

Community Detection. Community detection amounts to one of the most enduring themes in network science [12]. Due to complexity of real-world networks and inconsistencies among the intended uses of communities, there has not been a universally-accepted notion of a community structure. The closest to a generally-agreeable notion of communities is through Newman's *modularity* [22], which quantifies the level of deviation between the level of connectivity within communities and the expected level of connectivity in a null model that has the same degree distribution. Communities are defined as those that maximizes this deviation. However, there are known insufficiencies to this formulation such as the resolution limit [11]. Nevertheless, modularity-based community detection methods such as the Louvain method [2] are widely adopted due to their superior performance.

2 Togetherness Based on Structural Entropy

2.1 Network Integration and Togetherness

By a *network* we mean an undirected and unweighted graphs $G = (V, E)$. A *community structure* over a network G is a partition of the node set V into a collection of subsets $\{C_1, C_2, \ldots, C_L\}$, called *communities*, where $\cup_{i=1}^{k} C_i = V$ and $\bigwedge_{i \neq j} C_i \cap C_j = \varnothing$. We need the following notions: N_v denotes the *neighborhood* of $v \in V$, d_v denotes the *degree* $|N_v|$ of a node $v \in V$, ν_i denotes the *volume* $\sum_{v \in C_i} d_v$ of C_i where $1 \leq i \leq L$, g_i denotes $|\{\{v, u\} \in E \mid v \in C_i, u \in V \backslash C_i\}|$. In general, if a community structure is given as input, we assume each community induces a densely-connected subgraph of G that is sparsely linked to other communities.

Network integration is a process that introduces a sequence of new edges to the graph to improve togetherness. More formally, fix two communities C_i, C_j, the process iteratively adds edges $e_1, e_2, \ldots$ that connect members of C_i with members of C_j. Our goal is to add as few edges as possible before $C_i \cup C_j$ can be regarded as a single community (as testified by running different community detection algorithms). Figure 1 illustrates an example of network integration using Zachary's karate club[1], a standard benchmark dataset for community detection. Communities in the graphs are identified using the Louvain method. It is seen that nodes are originally separated into four communities (as shown in different colors). After establishing 9 new edges (shown in red) between the communities in blue and in purple, a new community is formed that contains members from both original communities (shown on the right).

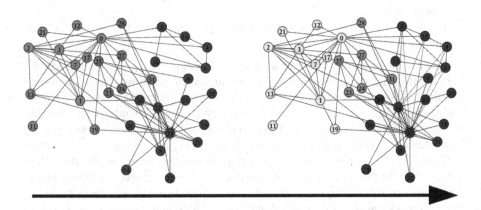

Fig. 1. Integrating two communities in Zachary's karate club network. After adding 9 edges between the blue and purple community, the two communities integrate as validated by the Louvain algorithm. (Color figure online)

---

[1] http://www-personal.umich.edu/~mejn/netdata/.

2.2 Structural Entropy

To give a formal definition of the problem, it is necessary to fix a notion of community. Here, we invoke structural information theory. The ability of quantify information embodied in structures has been a "grand challenge in the half-a-century-old computer science" as asserted by Brooks in [5]. For community detection, it has been conjectured that entropy-based methods would play a major role [9]. Many notions of entropy are defined on graphs [1,4,10,18], all of which are essentially Shannon entropy applied to different types of distributions, which measures many aspects of the graph but not about encoding of the graph structure itself and certainly not about a community structure.

Towards building a structural information theory, Li and Pan developed a framework in [15] to quantify structure information of graphs. We adopt this framework in this paper. Different from earlier notions of structural entropy, the framework by Li and Pan proposes a hierarchical structure to represent a graph G, with the root of the tree (top-most level) being the entire graph, the next level being the different communities that partition G which form the children of the root, and the level below that being sub-communities that partition a community, and so on, where each level downwards represent a collection of sets of nodes that forms a partition of the set above it. The leaves of this tree represent singleton node sets, i.e., individual nodes in the graph G. We call this hierarchy an *encoding tree* of G. At each level of this hierarchy, a graph encoding scheme is defined. We interpret Li and Pan's framework as follows which is different from their original description. Let $G = (V, E)$ be a graph with communities $\mathcal{P} = \{C_1, \ldots, C_L\}$. We study two questions:

- The first inquires about the minimum description length of G *without* community structure.
- The second inquires about the minimum description length of G *with* community structure.

For the first question, we consider a depth-1 encoding tree $\mathcal{T}_1$ where all children of the root are singleton nodes (hence no community information). In this scenario a *one-dimensional coding function* is a mapping $f \colon V \to \{0, 1\}^\star$ that assigns every leaf of the tree, i.e., a node in V, to a binary codeword. Under this encoding, an edge $\{v, u\} \in E$ has codeword $f(v)f(u)$ (for some fixed order between v, u). Now consider a codeword of the graph G by listing the codewords of all edges in G as $f(v_1)f(u_1), f(v_2)f(u_2), \ldots$ (every edge appears once and the order does not matter). In this encoding, every node $v \in V$ occurs exactly d_v times, among $2|E|$ node occurrences in total. It is thus reasonable to seek a coding function f that produces the shortest length description of all edges. Shannon entropy gives the lowerbound on the average length of nodes, which we call *one-dimensional structural entropy* of G. This value is our answer to the first goal.

Definition 1 [15]. *The* 1D *structural entropy of* G *is*

$$\mathcal{H}^1(G) = -\sum_{i=1}^{n} \frac{d_i}{2m} \cdot \log_2 \frac{d_i}{2m}. \tag{1}$$

For the second question, we consider a depth-2 encoding tree $\mathcal{T}_2$ where the children of the root denote communities $C_1, \ldots, C_L$, and the leaves (i.e., individual nodes) are children of their corresponding communities. In this case, a *two-dimensional coding function* is a pair of mappings $f_1: V \to \{0,1\}^*$ and $f_2: \mathcal{P} \to \{0,1\}^*$. In other words, f_1 assigns a codeword to every node in G and f_2 assigns a codeword to every community in $\mathcal{P}$. An edge $\{v,u\} \in E$ under this coding function can be considered as the shortest path that goes from the leaf v to leaf u on the tree:

- if u,v belong to the same community C_i, then this shortest path simply goes from v to C_i, and then from C_i to u. Thus we use $\langle\{v,u\}\rangle = f_1(v)f_1(u)$ to code this edge.
- if $u \in C_i$ and $v \in C_j$, then this shortest path goes from v to C_i, to the root, then to C_j, and finally to u. Thus we use $\langle\{v,u\}\rangle = f_1(v)f_2(C_i)f(C_j)f(u)$ to code this edge $\{v,u\}$.

Since the communities are explicitly coded in this scheme, the codeword $f_1(v)$ for each node can be made within its own community C_i. Thus the shortest $f_1(v)$ has expected length $\log_2 \frac{d_v}{\nu_i}$. When coding the community C_i, one also takes into account the frequency that a node belongs to C_i occurs in the list of all edges, and thus the shortest codeword of C_i has expected length $\log_2 \frac{\nu_i}{2|E|}$. Summing up, we define the two-dimensional structural entropy as our answer to the second question:

Definition 2 [15]. *The* 2D structural entropy $\mathcal{H}^{\mathcal{P}}(G)$ *is*

$$\sum_{j=1}^{L} \left[-\sum_{v_i \in C_j} \frac{d_i}{2|E|} \log_2 \frac{d_i}{\nu_j} - \frac{g_j}{2|E|} \log_2 \frac{\nu_j}{2|E|} \right]. \tag{2}$$

Here, $\mathcal{H}^{\mathcal{P}}(G)$ captures the average number of bits to encode nodes in E with the presence of community structure $\mathcal{P} = \{C_1, C_2, C_3, \ldots, C_L\}$. It is easy to see that $\mathcal{H}^1(G) \geq \mathcal{H}^{\mathcal{P}}(G)$ for any partition $\mathcal{P}$. Furthermore, $\mathcal{H}^1(G) = \mathcal{H}^{\mathcal{P}}(G)$ if and only if either $\mathcal{P} = \{V\}$ or $\mathcal{P} = \cup_{v \in V}\{\{v\}\}$.

2.3   Togetherness Improvement Through Entropy

Informally speaking, $\mathcal{H}^1(G)$ and $\mathcal{H}^{\mathcal{P}}(G)$ can be viewed as the amount of uncertainty within a graph before and after community detection, respectively. It is thus natural to compute the information gain as the amount of information revealed by the community structure $\mathcal{P}$.

Definition 3. *The* information gain *of* G *given community structure* $\mathcal{P}$ *is*

$$\rho^{\mathcal{P}}(G) = (\mathcal{H}^1(G) - \mathcal{H}^{\mathcal{P}}(G))/\mathcal{H}^1(G). \tag{3}$$

We are now ready to formally define the problem that we aim to solve in the paper. Suppose our goal is to integrate the two communities C_1 and C_2 in $\mathcal{P}$ by iteratively adding edges. In every step, we would like to add a new edge

$\{v, u\}$ such that the community structure $\mathcal{P}' = \{C_1 \cup C_2, C_3, C_4, \ldots, C_L\}$ has the maximum information gain. Let $C_1 \otimes C_2 = \{\{v, u\} \mid v \in C_1, u \in C_2\}$ and $G \oplus \{u, v\}$ be $(V, E \cup \{\{u, v\}\})$. The *togetherness improvement problem* seeks to

$$\text{Maximize}_{\{v,u\} \in (C_1 \otimes C_2) \setminus E} \; \rho^{\mathcal{P}}(G \oplus \{v, u\}). \tag{4}$$

3   The TIE Algorithm

Solving the problem above brute-force takes time $O(|C_1||C_2|)$ which is inefficient if the communities are large and the procedure needs to iterate. We now present a faster algorithm with a simple observation: namely that one can maximize $\rho^{\mathcal{P}}(G \oplus \{u, v\})$ simply by comparing the degrees of nodes in the communities.

Let $G = (V, E)$ be an connected undirected graph, $P = (C_1 \cup C_2, C_3, \ldots, C_L)$ be the original community structure of $G = (V, E)$ and d_v is the degree of $v \in V$. Assume C_1 and C_2 are the communities to be merged, then the expected community structure is $P = (C_1 \cup C_2, C_3, \ldots, C_L)$ We say that a non-edge $\{u, v\} \in C_1 \otimes C_2$ is RE-Max for $C_1 \otimes C_2$ if $\rho^P(G \oplus \{u, v\}) \geq \rho^P(G \oplus \{x, y\})$ for any non-edge $\{x, y\} \in C_1 \otimes C_2$. For the candidate non-edge $\{u, v\}$, we have the following max-degree theorem about RE-Max:

Theorem 1 (max-degree principle). *If $\{u, v\} \in (C_1 \otimes C_2) \setminus E$ is an optimal solution to the togetherness improvement problem(RE-Max), then $d_u \geq d_{u'}$ for any node $u' \in C_1$ with $\{u', v\} \in (C_1 \otimes C_2) \setminus E$, and $d_v \geq d_{v'}$ for any node $v' \in C_2$ with $\{u, v'\} \in (C_1 \otimes C_2) \setminus E$.*

Proof. If there exists a $\{u', v\} \in (C_1 \otimes C_2) \setminus E$ satisfying $d_{u'} > d_u$ and $\rho^{\mathcal{P}'}(G \oplus \{u', v\}) > \rho^{\mathcal{P}'}(G \oplus \{u, v\})$. By (1) and (2), the value of $\mathcal{H}^1(H) - \mathcal{H}^P(H)$ when $H = G \oplus \{u, v\}$ or $H = G \oplus \{u', v\}$ both equal to

$$-\sum_{j \neq 1,2} \frac{\nu_j - g_j}{2|E| + 2} \log_2 \frac{\nu_j}{2|E| + 2} - \sum_{j \in \{1,2\}} \frac{\nu_j - g_j}{2|E| + 2} \log_2 \frac{\nu_j + 1}{2|E| + 2}.$$

Then Definition 3 implies that $\mathcal{H}^1(G \oplus \{u, v\}) < \mathcal{H}^1(G \oplus \{u', v\})$. Note that $\mathcal{H}^1(G \oplus \{u, v\}) - \mathcal{H}^1(G \oplus \{u', v\}) = -\frac{1}{2|E|+2}(F(d_u) - F(d_{u'}))$ where $F \colon \mathbb{R} \to \mathbb{R}$ is defined by $F(x) = (x + 1)\log_2(x + 1) - x \log_2 x$. Since F is monotonically increasing and $d_{u'} > d_u$, we have $\mathcal{H}^1(G \oplus \{u, v\}) > \mathcal{H}^1(G \oplus \{u', v\})$, contradiction with the assumption. Therefore $d_u \geq d_{u'}$ for any node $x \in C_2$ and $\{x, v\} \notin E$. The same proof can be applied to d_v.

Denote $\{u, v\} \in C_1 \otimes C_2$ or $\{u, v\} \in C_2 \otimes C_1$. We define a non-edge $\{u, v\} \in C_1 \& C_2$ as a critical edge for u if v has the maximal degree among all non-edge $\{u, y\} \in C_1 \& C_2$. From the max-degree principle in Theorem 1, if a non-edge u, v is RE-Max, the edge must be a critical edge, then we only need search RE-Max among the critical edges $\{u, v\}$ for $u \in C_1 \cup C_2$. The max-degree principle asserts that any new edge $\{u, v\}$ that amounts to an optimal solution to the togetherness improvement problem must satisfy that $\{u, v\} \in Cand$, where $Cand$ is a set of critical edges. With this edge set, we can implement this algorithm iteratively. Based on this idea, we refer to this algorithm as **T**ogetherness **I**mprovement thru **E**ntropy (TIE):

ALGORITHM 1. Togetherness improvement algorithm TIE

---

input: $G = (V, E)$, budget k, expect community stucture $P = (C_1 \cup C_2, C_3, \dots, C_L)$
output: a non-edge set E'
1:   $E' = \phi$, $\rho_{max} = 0$
2:   Create a candidate edge set $Cand = \{(x, y) \mid x \in C_1 \cup C_2\}$ so that $\{x, y\}$ is the critical non-edge of $C_1 \& C_2$
3:   **for** $i = 1 \longrightarrow k$ **do**
4:      **for** $\{u, v\} \in Cand$ **do**
5:         **if** $\rho^P(G \oplus \{u, v\}) > \rho_{max}$ **then**
6:            $u^* \leftarrow u, v^* \leftarrow v, \rho_{max} = \rho^P(G \oplus \{u, v\})$
7:         **end if**
8:      **end for**
9:      $E' = E' \cup \{u^*, v^*\}$, $E = E \cup \{u^*, v^*\}$
10:     $\rho_{max} = 0$, update $Cand$ by function UPDATE
11: **end for**
12: **return** E'
13:
14: **function** UPDATE($Cand, \{u^*, v^*\}$)
15:     **for** $\{u, v\} \in Cand$ **do**
16:        **if** $u = u^*$ or $v = v^*$ **then**
17:           recalculate critical edge $\{u, v'\}$ for u
18:           $Cand = Cand \cup \{u, v'\} \setminus \{u, v\}$
19:        **else if** $\delta \{u, v^*\} = 0$ and $d_v < d_{v^*}$ and $\{u, v^*\} \notin E$ **then**
20:           $Cand = Cand \cup \{u, v^*\} \setminus \{u, v\}$
21:        **else if** $\delta \{u, u^*\} = 0$ and $d_u < d_{u^*}$ and $\{u, u^*\} \notin E$ **then**
22:           $Cand = Cand \cup \{u, u^*\} \setminus \{u, v\}$
23:        **end if**
24:     **end for**
25:     **return** $Cand$
26: **end function**

To simple, we denote $\delta \{u, v\} = 1$ if u, v belong to the same community and $\delta \{u, v\} = 1$ if they belong to different communities in Algorithm 1. This Algorithm contains two main steps: the computing step and the update step. In the computing step (line 4–8), TIE computes information gain $\rho^P(G \oplus \{v, u\})$ for all the candidate edges to search the maximal one RE-Max. Since we only save one critical edge for each node $u \in C_1 \cup C_2$, then this step takes at most $|C_1| + |C_2|$. times. In the update step (line 14–26), TIE will update the candidate edges. Specially, if u is the endpoint of the optimal edge $\{u^*, v^*\}$ in computing step, the function recalculate the critical edge for u, and if the remain candidate edge is not critical, replace one of the endpoint with u^* or v^*. This step takes at most $2(|C_1| + |C_2|)$. It means that the procedure of adding one edge takes time $O(|C_1| + |C_2|)$, it's far better than brute-force implementation that takes time $O(|C_1||C_2|)$.

Therefore, by iterating k times, the time complexity of TIE is $O(|C_1||C_2| + k(|C_1| + |C_2|))$, where $|C_1||C_2|$ is the time by creating a candidate edge set.

4   Experiment

We evaluate our solution to the togetherness improvement problem aiming to answer three questions: 1) how does TIE compare with existing benchmark w.r.t. improving togetherness when evaluated using an established community detection algorithm? and 2) How efficient is the TIE algorithm?

Table 1. The key statistics of real networks

Name	$|V|$	$|E|$	$(|C_1|, |E(C_1)|)$	$(|C_2|, |E(C_2)|)$
filmtrust	874	1853	(68, 94)	(61, 137)
email	1133	5451	(121, 345)	(127, 348)
cora	2708	5278	(205, 458)	(196, 312)
facebook	14113	52309	(114, 402)	(107, 364)

4.1   Experimental Settings

Datasets. We answer the questions above by performing network integration on real-world and synthetic datasets. Let E_i denote the edge set inside community C_i for $i \in \{1, 2\}$. Table 1 provides key statistics of the used real-world dataset: **filmtrust** (http://konect.cc/networks/librec-filmtrust-trust/) is the user-user trust network of the FilmTrust project, **email** (http://konect.cc/networks/arenas-email/) is the email communication network at the University Rovira i Virgili in Spain, **cora** (https://paperswithcode.com/dataset/cora) is the citation network of 2708 scientific publications, and **facebook** (http://networkrepository.com/fb-pages-company.php) is the "mutually-liked" network among facebook pages. We also apply the well-established *LFR model* to generate a number of synthetic networks [14] for which Table 2 lists key statistics. The parameter K of the LFR model refers to the desired average degree and μ the fraction of inter-community edges. The real-world graphs do not have a specified community structure. We therefore we choose $\mathcal{P}$ produced by the community detection algorithm. Due to space limitation, we display our results only using the Louvain method due to its prevalence use in literature. Results for different community detection algorithms will be provided in an extended version of the paper.

Table 2. The key statistics of synthetic networks generated by LFR

$|V|$	$|E|$	K	μ	$(|C_1|, |E_1|)$	$(|C_2|, |E_2|)$
100	261	5	0.8	(14, 22)	(20, 36)
500	3059	15	0.8	(78, 214)	(83, 201)
1000	6463	15	0.8	(139, 349)	(141, 372)
10000	299115	8	0.95	(944, 5776)	(931, 5664)

Benchmark Algorithms. Three edge creation strategies are chosen as benchmarks. All these algorithms were adopted in [21] where CtrPer has demonstrated effectiveness:

- **Random:** Adding edges randomly between C_1 and C_2;
- **Min-deg:** Adding edge $\{u, v\}$ if u has the minimal degree in C_1 and v has the minimal degree among all non-edge $\{u, v\} \in C_1 \otimes C_2$.
- **Max-bet:** adding edge $\{u, v\}$ if u has the maximal betweenness in C_1 and v has the maximal betweenness among all non-edge $\{u, v\} \in C_1 \otimes C_2$.
- **CtrPer:** add edges by optimizing $\forall$-togetherness in network integration.

Performance Index. Let the edge set E' be a set of added edges and $\mathcal{P}' = \{C_1', C_2', C_3', \ldots, C_{L'}'\}$ be the community structure detected on $G \oplus E'$. Denote

$$S_{\max}(\mathcal{P}') = \max \left\{ \frac{|C \cap C_y'|}{\sqrt{|C| \times |C_y'|}} \mid C_y' \in \mathcal{P}' \right\} \tag{5}$$

Then $S_{\max}(\mathcal{P}')$ measures the similarity between $C = C_1 \cup C_2$ and communities identified. A higher $S_{\max}$ value indicate better performance. We also consider F1-score which quantifiers the chance that edges in C_1 and C_2 still lie in the combined community $C = C_1 \cup C_2$ [23].

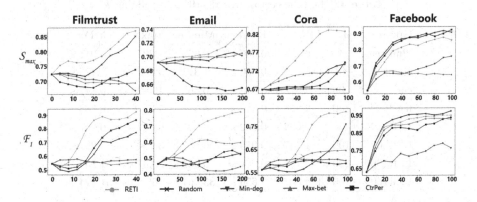

Fig. 2. Results on real world network. The horizontal axis indicates the number of new edges added to each graph. Each node is the average over 100 runs.

4.2   Results and Analysis

Togetherness Improvement. Figure 2 compares performance to togetherness improvement as more edges are added: As more edges are added, both S_{max} and F1-score increases for the TIE algorithm. TIE clearly outperforms the benchmarks w.r.t. both metrics on graphs *filmtrust*, *email* and *cora*, and comparable with the best strategy on *facebook*. On *facebook*, several algorithm all quickly achieve good performance and therefore the advantage of TIE is not clearly shown. On synthetic LFR networks with 100, 500, 1000, 10000 nodes, we add a certain ratio of edges between the communities. Table 3 lists the resulting S_{max} scores. TIE clearly outperforms benchmarks in all cases. Max-bet was not shown due to its high computation cost and lack of space.

Efficiency. Table 4 lists the running time versus number of edges added. Each value of time is the average of 50 repeated experiments. Random adding edges uses the shortest time. TIE runs in reasonable time for all cases.

Table 3. The resulting S_{max} index of network integration on LFR networks of various sizes

	TIE			Random			Min-deg			CtrPer		
LFR	10%	20%	30%	10%	20%	30%	10%	20%	30%	10%	20%	30%
100	**0.68**	**0.72**	**0.78**	0.61	0.64	0.70	0.58	0.62	0.70	0.59	0.63	0.71
500	**0.45**	**0.57**	**0.64**	0.38	0.41	0.47	0.39	0.45	0.55	0.37	0.40	0.47
1000	**0.39**	**0.48**	**0.56**	0.35	0.39	0.45	0.38	0.43	0.51	0.34	0.37	0.41
10000	**0.20**	**0.28**	**0.37**	0.19	0.19	0.19	0.19	0.23	0.27	**0.20**	0.21	0.21

Table 4. The time cost of five algorithm by adding E'

Graph	$|E'|$	TIE	Random	Min-deg	Max-bet	CtrPer
filmtrust	40	0.148 s	0.006 s	0.032 s	1.387 s	0.041 s
email	200	6.838 s	0.050 s	1.314 s	32.473 s	2.425 s
cora	100	2.628 s	0.042 s	0.565 s	109.29 s	0.817 s
facebook	100	2.408 s	0.349 s	0.645 s	1358.8 s	0.788 s
LFR100	50	0.033 s	0.002 s	0.005 s	0.027 s	0.007 s
LFR500	100	1.147 s	0.016 s	0.206 s	3.830 s	0.297 s
LFR1000	200	4.744 s	0.067 s	0.951 s	23.379 s	1.234 s
LFR10000	100	114.80 s	2.656 s	33.061 s	4657.9 s	51.424 s

5 Conclusion and Future Work

This paper studies the togetherness improvement problem that aims to integrate communities in a social network by employing tools from structural information theory. The integration of communities can be facilitated by structural entropy where information gain provides the key to improving togetherness. We design an efficient TIE algorithm for the task which is validated on both real-world and synthetic datasets. Future work includes extending the problem and method to directed, attributed, or weighted networks as well as considering other strategies, e.g., rewiring for network integration.

References

1. Anand, K., Bianconi, G.: Entropy measures for networks: toward an information theory of complex topologies. Phys. Rev. E 80(4), 045102 (2009)
2. Blondel, V.D., Guillaume, J.L., Lambiotte, R., Lefebvre, E.: Fast unfolding of communities in large networks. J. Stat. Mech: Theory Exp. 2008(10), P10008 (2008)
3. Borgatti, S.P., Everett, M.G.: A graph-theoretic perspective on centrality. Soc. Netw. 28(4), 466–484 (2006)
4. Braunstein, S.L., Ghosh, S., Mansour, T., Severini, S., Wilson, R.C.: Some families of density matrices for which separability is easily tested. Phys. Rev. A 73(1), 012320 (2006)
5. Brooks, F.P., Jr.: Three great challenges for half-century-old computer science. J. ACM (JACM) 50(1), 25–26 (2003)
6. Bruhn, J.: The concept of social cohesion. In: Bruhn, J. (ed.) The Group Effect, pp. 31–48. Springer, Boston (2009). https://doi.org/10.1007/978-1-4419-0364-8_2
7. Cai, Y., Zheng, H., Liu, J., Yan, B., Su, H., Liu, Y.: Balancing the pain and gain of hobnobbing: utility-based network building over atributed social networks. In: Proceedings of the 17th International Conference on Autonomous Agents and MultiAgent Systems, pp. 193–201 (2018)
8. Chen, Q., Su, H., Liu, J., Yan, B., Zheng, H., Zhao, H.: In pursuit of social capital: upgrading social circle through edge rewiring. In: Shao, J., Yiu, M.L., Toyoda, M., Zhang, D., Wang, W., Cui, B. (eds.) APWeb-WAIM 2019. LNCS, vol. 11641, pp. 207–222. Springer, Cham (2019). https://doi.org/10.1007/978-3-030-26072-9_15
9. Chunaev, P.: Community detection in node-attributed social networks: a survey. Comput. Sci. Rev. 37, 100286 (2020)
10. Dehmer, M.: Information processing in complex networks: graph entropy and information functionals. Appl. Math. Comput. 201(1–2), 82–94 (2008)
11. Fortunato, S., Barthelemy, M.: Resolution limit in community detection. Proc. Natl. Acad. Sci. 104(1), 36–41 (2007)
12. Fortunato, S., Lancichinetti, A.: Community detection algorithms: a comparative analysis: invited presentation, extended abstract. In: Proceedings of the Fourth International ICST Conference on Performance Evaluation Methodologies and Tools, pp. 1–2 (2009)
13. Jiang, H., Carroll, J.M.: Social capital, social network and identity bonds: a reconceptualization. In: Proceedings of the Fourth International Conference on Communities and Technologies, pp. 51–60 (2009)

14. Lancichinetti, A., Fortunato, S., Radicchi, F.: Benchmark graphs for testing community detection algorithms. Phys. Rev. E **78**(4), 046110 (2008)
15. Li, A., Pan, Y.: Structural information and dynamical complexity of networks. IEEE Trans. Inf. Theory **62**(6), 3290–3339 (2016)
16. Liu, J., Wei, Z.: Network, popularity and social cohesion: a game-theoretic approach. In: Proceedings of the AAAI Conference on Artificial Intelligence, vol. 31 (2017)
17. Liu, Y., et al.: From local to global norm emergence: dissolving self-reinforcing substructures with incremental social instruments. In: International Conference on Machine Learning, pp. 6871–6881. PMLR (2021)
18. Liu, Y., Liu, J., Zhang, Z., Zhu, L., Li, A.: REM: from structural entropy to community structure deception. Adv. Neural. Inf. Process. Syst. **32**, 12938–12948 (2019)
19. Moskvina, A., Liu, J.: How to build your network? A structural analysis. arXiv preprint arXiv:1605.03644 (2016)
20. Moskvina, A., Liu, J.: Integrating networks of equipotent nodes. In: Nguyen, H.T.T., Snasel, V. (eds.) CSoNet 2016. LNCS, vol. 9795, pp. 39–50. Springer, Cham (2016). https://doi.org/10.1007/978-3-319-42345-6_4
21. Moskvina, A., Liu, J.: Togetherness: an algorithmic approach to network integration. In: 2016 IEEE/ACM International Conference on Advances in Social Networks Analysis and Mining (ASONAM), pp. 223–230. IEEE (2016)
22. Newman, M.E.: Modularity and community structure in networks. Proc. Natl. Acad. Sci. **103**(23), 8577–8582 (2006)
23. Shalev-Shwartz, S., Ben-David, S.: Understanding Machine Learning: From Theory to Algorithms. Cambridge University Press, Cambridge (2014)
24. Tang, Y., Liu, J., Chen, W., Zhang, Z.: Establishing connections in a social network. In: Geng, X., Kang, B.-H. (eds.) PRICAI 2018. LNCS (LNAI), vol. 11012, pp. 1044–1057. Springer, Cham (2018). https://doi.org/10.1007/978-3-319-97304-3_80
25. Vitak, J., Ellison, N.B., Steinfield, C.: The ties that bond: re-examining the relationship between Facebook use and bonding social capital. In: 2011 44th Hawaii International Conference on System Sciences, pp. 1–10. IEEE (2011)
26. Yan, B., Chen, Y., Liu, J.: Dynamic relationship building: exploitation versus exploration on a social network. In: Bouguettaya, A., et al. (eds.) WISE 2017. LNCS, vol. 10569, pp. 75–90. Springer, Cham (2017). https://doi.org/10.1007/978-3-319-68783-4_6
27. Yan, B., Liu, Y., Liu, J., Cai, Y., Su, H., Zheng, H.: From the periphery to the center: information brokerage in an evolving network. arXiv preprint arXiv:1805.00751 (2018)
28. Zhao, H., Su, H., Chen, Y., Liu, J., Zheng, H., Yan, B.: A reinforcement learning approach to gaining social capital with partial observation. In: Nayak, A.C., Sharma, A. (eds.) PRICAI 2019. LNCS (LNAI), vol. 11670, pp. 113–117. Springer, Cham (2019). https://doi.org/10.1007/978-3-030-29908-8_9

Blockchain-Based Group Key Agreement

Caifei Shen[⊠]

Beijing Institute of Technology, Beijing, China
caifeishen@bit.edu.cn

Abstract. Blockchain can provide trusted ledgers on distributed architecture without the help of any central authority. Since all the transactions are saved in the ledgers, they can be obtained in public. By using the transactions, this paper first proposes a blockchain-based Diffie-Hellman key agreement (BDKA) protocol. Then, a blockchain-based group key agreement (BGKA) protocol is further proposed. In addition, both BDKA and BGKA protocols are implemented in the Bitcoin system. The performance of protocol execution and transaction fee are analyzed in the experiments.

Keywords: Blockchain · Key agreement · Group key agreement

1 Introduction

Blockchain technology has been widely used in many industrial applications. For instances, it enables the Internet of Vehicles to build secure communication groups in vehicular ad-hot networks. It is applied to protect video copyright in the process of video-streaming distribution. It is also praised for reliably balancing a user and her neighbors' electricity supply and demand in smart grid. Moreover, blockchain technology is innately welcome in the application of group communication since the ledger is public for all users in public blockchain and all authorized members in consortium blockchain. However, the most common blockchain applications mainly focus on maintaining data integrity and non-repudiation by using the characteristics of the publicity and immutability of the ledger. This paper tries to extend blockchain applications to support key exchange and group key exchange. The motivation is because the ledger in blockchain can be naturally regarded as a broadcasting communication channel [10]. Suppose a secret key can be exchanged by the transactions saved in the ledger, it can be used as the pre-shared key to build a covert communication channel. Messages can be secretly delivered among users when combining the pre-shared key with some blockchain-based covert encoding and decoding schemes [10]. It can be used as a forensic evidence in the consortium or even public as the ledger is nearly impossible to be tampered in reality. It can also be used to construct a secure blockchain-based communication channel for group members [10].

This paper is supported by National Natural Science Foundation of China No. 62172040, No. U1836212, No. 61872041.

S. Deng et al. (Eds.): MobiCASE 2021, LNICST 434, pp. 99–111, 2022.
https://doi.org/10.1007/978-3-030-99203-3_7

In recent years, several works designed group key agreement protocols on blockchains. For instances, McCorry et al. [11] applied Bitcoin to achieve authenticated Diffie-Hellman-based key agreement (DHKA). Specifically, the Bitcoin Core client was modified to adding the DHKA procedure as remote commands. The procedure commands are stored and executed off-chain. In [3], Thanh Bui et al. presented a two-party key exchange protocol that uses the global consistency property of blockchains. [7] used Proof of Work (POW)-based public ledger and Delegated Proof of Stake (DPoS)-based public ledger to create a key tree and store the list of authorized group members. The POW-based mechanism is different from that of Bitcoin, because the block generation is not competitive. Although blockchain-based group key exchange have been attempted, to the best of our knowledge, the existing works usually require to modify the executable software or the consensus mechanism.

The main contribution of this paper is summarized as below.

(1) A blockchain-based key agreement protocol and a blockchain-based group key agreement protocol are proposed without requiring to modify the existing blockchain system, such as the executable software or the consensus mechanism.
(2) A dynamically joining or leaving scheme is designed for the blockchain-based group key agreement protocol. New group members are unable to obtain the historical group key, while left group members cannot compute the future's group key.
(3) An address update scheme with key update is provided for users when users would like to preserve her identity private. This scheme does not require to modify the existing blockchain system as well.

The rest of the paper is organized as follows. Section 2 reviews the related works. In Sect. 3, we introduce the preliminaries. Section 4 proposes group key agreement protocols. Section 5 analyses the security and the performance of the proposed protocol in the Bitcoin system. The conclusion is drawn in Sect. 6.

2   Related Works

Several studies have been focusing on establishing secure key agreement protocols based on blockchain systems. Most of the protocols were essentially designed based on the integrity, non-repudiation, and global consistency of the ledger in blockchain systems. For instances, McCorry et al. proposed two blockchain-based key agreement protocols under the hard mathematical assumptions of Elliptic Curve Diffie-Hellman (ECDH) [12] and the YAK zero knowledge proof-based key agreement protocol [8]. The protocols are implemented for Bitcoin users in post-transaction scenario. Specifically, the random nonce k_s used in the transaction signatures was taken to establish secret keys without requiring any Trusted Third Party (TTP). However, both protocols required to modify the Bitcoin client. Bui et al. [3] presented a family of key exchange protocols. These protocols used the global consistency of the public ledgers; therefore, every user can obtain the same messages to avoid the man-in-the-middle attack. However, these protocols need an out-of-band channel for sharing parameters, when public identities are not available.

For specific purpose, Zhang et al. [16] discussed a lightweight group key agreement protocol for the resource-limited internet of vehicles. In [2], a blockchain-based key agreement protocol was designed for smart grid to manage the group key in the Neighborhood Area Networks (NAN). However, they have not sufficient consideration about dynamically joining and leaving for the members.

3 Preliminaries

In this section, we will briefly recall the Bitcoin system, and the existing group key exchange protocols. They are the preliminaries when designing our protocols presented in the next sections.

3.1 Data Format of Bitcoin Transactions

Bitcoin was proposed by Satoshi Nakamoto in 2008 [13], which is a digital cryptocurrency system that does not contain central financial institutions. It allows everyone to access a public ledger and to agree upon recording append-only changes on the ledger.

Bitcoin transactions are basic information units for users to communicate, forming by accounts, amount, signatures and other information. There are two types of Bitcoin transaction structures currently-the Bitcoin White Paper defined transactions and new Segregated Witness transactions-shown in Table 1.

Table 1. Bitcoin transactions' structure [1]

version	4 bytes	Transaction version number
*Marker	1 byte	0x00
*Flag	1 byte	0x01
tx_in count	varies	Number of inputs in this transaction
tx_in	varies	Transaction detail inputs
tx_out count	varies	Numbers of outputs in this transaction
tx_out	varies	Transaction-outputs
*Witness	varies	SigWit transaction witness data
lock_time	4 bytes	Unix epoch time or block number

Miners will collect the most recent set of transactions from the network to form a 'block'. This block is appended to the longest Bitcoin chain of blocks, including the hash pointer pointing to the previous block. The chain-like structure makes it generally believed that Bitcoin transaction information cannot be tampered with after 6 blocks confirming.

Early back in 2013, some Bitcoin ecosystem participants were trying to include bits of information into transactions so that they could take advantages of the irreversibility of the blockchain. Even Satoshi Nakamoto writed complaint about current bank system in Genesis Block. Doing this on the Bitcoin, someone encoded the transaction's script-Sig value to store extra information avoiding to alter the final result of running that script. Other ways were also presented, like using BTC value, outputs account, output addresses.

OP_RETURN is the Bitcoin script opcode, which also is the most direct way of placing extra data in transactions. To met this demand, the Bitcoin core-developers made Bitcoin v0.9.0 support that 40 bytes can be recorded by OP_RETURN transacitons. Then for Bitcoin v0.11.x, this ability upgraded to upto 80 bytes. So we are allowed to send less-than-80 bytes by a standard Bitcoin tansaction now, which is also one communication message in our scheme. Figure 1 highlights how transactions carry our communication information.

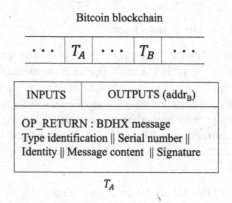

Fig. 1. Bitcoin blockchain and transactions' structure.

Bitcoin provides support to build standard OP_RETURN transaciton by developers making outputs to start with OP_RETURN opcode and to follow all the other consensus rules. Extra data can be appended to it, and these transacitons will be relayed and mined by Bitcoin nodes as usual. OP_RETURN transactions are not distinguished from ordinary transfer transacitons, and extra data written in will not be discarded or parsed by Bitcoin.

3.2 Group Key Agreement

The goal of group key agreement is to set up and maintain a shared secret key among the group members. It serves as a fundamental service for other security services. There are three kinds of methods to establish group key for user groups. One Method relies on a single entity (usually called key server) to generate and distribute keys to the group members. Another method dynamically selects group member to generate and distribute keys to other members in the group. The other method is called contributory group key agreement. This method requires each group member to contribute an equal share to the common group key. It can avoid the problems with the centralized trust and the single point of failure.

4 Protocols

In this section, we first propose a Blockchain-based Diffie-Hellman Key agreement (BDHA) protocol that can solve the challenge of key agreement and key update. We then extend the BDHA protocol from two-party to multiple-party, and present a blockchain-based group key agreement protocol. All of the notations and symbols are summarized in Table 2.

Table 2. Notations and symbols.

S	The secret session key
P	A prime number
A, B	Members in a key agreement protocol
N	The total number of members
$addr_A, addr_B$	The blockchain addresses of members
$addk_A, addk_B$	The private keys of members
K_{AB}	The pre-shared key between members A and B
M_i	The i-th group member where $i \in \{1, \ldots, N\}$
h	the height of a key tree
l	the level of a node located in a key tree
$\langle l, v \rangle$	The v-th node at level l in a key tree
T_i	The M_i's view of a key tree
$\hat{T}_i$	T_i's view of modified tree for member joining and leaving
$T_{\langle l,v \rangle}$	A subtree rooted at node $\langle l, v \rangle$
BK_i^*	set of M_i's blinded keys

4.1 A Blockchain-Based Two-Party Key Agreement Protocol

The Diffie-Hellman(DH) key agreement (DHKA) protocol [6] is the basis of most two-party communication protocols and multi-party communication protocols [14]. It allows two users to establish a secret key between two participants for subsequent encryption without revealing the key on the communication channel. This blockchain-based key exchange protocol starts from that protocol correspondingly.

The following is a brief description of how two members negotiate a secret session key via transactions. In order to exchange a secret session key, A and B have to agree on a prime number P and a generator G. After agreeing on P and G, A and B randomly pick up temporarily private keys $K_A = a, K_B = b$, respectively. The temporarily public keys of A and B are aG and bG, correspondingly. Coming to the blockchain part, both A and B send a transaction after embedding each temporarily public key. Then A and B records users' names with their blockchain addresses in use. After a transaction sends from A/B's blockchain address to B/A's blockchain address. B/A will download it from the ledger, checks the validity and extracts the temporarily public key. Eventually, A and B can calculate the secret session key independently.

$$S = \left(G^b\right)^a \ mod \ P = \left(G^a\right)^b \ mod \ P = G^{ab} \ mod \ P \tag{1}$$

Here, since the temporarily public keys are permanent recorded on the blockchain, any user can obtain them. But the temporarily private key generation is executed locally. Thus, it will not be broadcasted with transactions.

From the viewpoint of the adversary, she is negligible to compute S, because she has neither learned a nor b from any of the transactions. Hence, as long as the discrete logarithm problem is hard, the adversary is difficult to get the secret session key. By the blockchain, since the adversary is also difficult to generate a valid transaction for any legitimate users, the active attack is also difficult to be launched.

The Blockchain-based Two-party Key Agreement Protocol

step 1: A confirms parameters g, p, B and her Blockchain address.

step 2: A randomly generates a temporarily private key a and computes the temporarily public key aG.

step 3: A sends a transaction to B for sending her temporarily public key aG to B.

$$A \xrightarrow[\quad A:aG \quad]{} B$$

step 4: When B receives this transaction and calculates secret session key S.

step 5: B sends a transaction back to A with his temporarily public key bG.

$$A \xleftarrow[\quad B:bG \quad]{} B$$

step 6: When receiving a transaction from B, A computes the secret key S.

We implement the protocol in the Bitcoin system. Specifically, the Bitcoin system provides developers with the technical support for coding the Output script of each transaction with the OP_RETURN opcode. The OP_RETURN opcode is followed by the position where the data can be written without having any impact for the validity of the transaction. The written data is also known as NULL DATA. Bitcoin transactions with NULL DATA can be relayed and mined by Bitcoin miners, which are difficult to be distinguished from ordinary transfer transactions. In addition, Bitcoin network will not parse the protocol data that we write in the fragment of OP_RETURN. Therefore, we can embed the parameters and temporarily public keys in this fragment. After encoding the protocol messages into the fragment of OP_RETURN. It can be broadcasted in the ledger by the Bitcoin network, as shown in Fig. 2.

4.2 A Blockchain-Based Group Key Agreement Protocol

For the case of group communication, setting up and maintaining a secret session key among group members can be expanded from the two-party protocol. The Tree-based Group DH (TGDH) protocol is the first group key agreement protocol based on a tree and the DH protocol. Applying the TGDH protocol to the blockchain, each user generates her own key pair: temporarily private key and temporarily public key. The temporarily private key is known to herself, and the temporarily public key is public to other

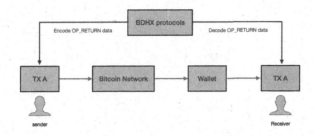

Fig. 2. The process of the blockchain-based two-party key agreement protocols

group members. Users can use their own blockchain addresses to send transactions carrying protocol messages to other users, while other users can extract the messages sent to themselves from the received transactions.

For each group member, they record a mapping table for member names with their blockchain addresses, so that they can identify members from their transactions. Here is a challenge that has been solved. That is, a leaved member can obtain the transaction addresses of all members of the group, and can monitor the remaining members in the group in the later period. Through information such as the number of transactions and frequency, the leaving members can learn about the changes and activities of the group members. Information such as frequency may even be used for data analysis to cluster addresses and expose the privacy of group member. Therefore, in this protocol, when a user joins or leaves, the group key is forced to be updated and the addresses have to be updated at the same time.

The protocol description is listed as below:

- The key tree structure is shown in the Fig. 3. Here, the root of the tree is located at level l_0, and the lowest leaf node is located at level h. Since each node in a binary tree is either a leaf node or the parent node of one or two nodes. Nodes can be represented by $\langle l, v \rangle$, and there are at most $2l$ nodes in layer l. Each node $\langle l, v \rangle$ is associated with the temporarily private key $K \langle l, v \rangle$ and the temporarily public key $BK \langle l, v \rangle$, $BK \langle l, v \rangle = f(K \langle l, v \rangle)$. The $f(\cdot)$ function can be determined due to the concrete key exchange protocol.
- Assuming that a leaf node $\langle l, v \rangle$ represents the member M_i, node $\langle l, v \rangle$ will have the private key $K \langle l, v \rangle$ of member M_i, and it can get the every key along the path from $\langle l, v \rangle$ to $\langle 0, 0 \rangle$, this set is called KEY_i^*.
- As shown in the Fig. 3, if the key tree that can be viewed from the perspective of M_2 is called T_2, then M_2 can get all the keys of KEY_2^* $\{K \langle 3, 1 \rangle, K \langle 2, 0 \rangle, K \langle 0, 0 \rangle, K \langle 0, 0 \rangle\}$, and all temporarily public keys $\{BK \langle 0, 0 \rangle, BK \langle 1, 0 \rangle, BK \langle 1, 1 \rangle, \ldots, BK \langle 3, 7 \rangle\}$ of T_2.
- $K \langle 0, 0 \rangle$ is the secret group key that is negotiated by the group members, and the group session key can be derived from $K \langle 0, 0 \rangle$.
- If a member joins or leaves, all remaining members independently update the key tree structure. Since all the changes are recorded on the ledger of the blockchain, all members who correctly execute the protocol can recompute identical key trees.

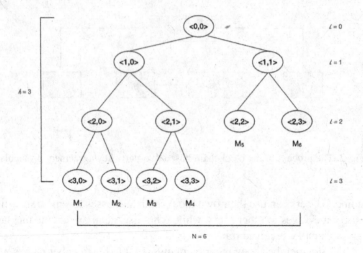

Fig. 3. The structure of the key tree

Any group member can be the initiator, which involves calculating intermediate keys and broadcasting to the group by the ledger. Each broadcast message contains the sender's viewpoint of the key tree that contains every key known for the sender. (The intermediate key will never be broadcasted.)

Member Joining. Assuming that the group has N members, $\{M_1, M_2, \ldots, M_n\}$, a new member M_{n+1} initiates the joining protocol by sending a transaction to group members' addresses that he knew. The transaction contains the joining request and his own temporarily public key. Each member will receive this transaction and determine the insertion point in the tree. The insertion point is the rightmost node at the lowest level to avoid increasing the height of the key tree. If the key tree is fully balanced, new members will join as the root node. The sponsor is the rightmost leaf in the sub-tree rooted at the inserted node, and it is the member representative of the group that negotiates the key with the joining or leaving members. Each member creates a new intermediate node and a new member node, and promotes the new intermediate node to the parent node of the insertion node and the new member node. After updating the key tree, all members except the sponsor wait. The sponsor updates its key and calculates a new group key because it knows all the temporarily public keys. Finally, the sponsor broadcasts a new tree containing all the temporarily public keys. All the members will update their tree accordingly and calculate a new group key. This group key tree will be recorded on the blockchain.

Figure 4 takes an example of the member M_4 joining a group where the sponsor M_3 performs the following actions:

1. Rename the node $\langle 1, 1 \rangle$ to $\langle 2, 2 \rangle$
2. Generate a new intermediate node $\langle 1, 1 \rangle$ and a new member node $\langle 2, 3 \rangle$
3. Promote $\langle 1, 1 \rangle$ as the parent node of $\langle 2, 2 \rangle$ and $\langle 2, 3 \rangle$

Since all members know $BK_{(2,3)}$ and $BK_{(1,0)}$, M_3 performs the step 1 and 2, but cannot compute the group key in the first round. Upon receiving the broadcasted temporarily public keys, every member can compute the new group key.

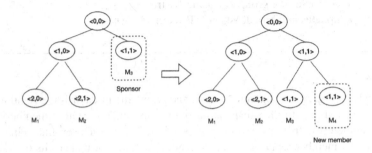

Fig. 4. A new member joins and key tree updates

To join a new member M_{n+1}, the transaction outputs do not have to include every group members, because the transactions on the blockchain are public for every member. M_{n+1} can send to certain members' addresses that he knows. They will allow group members to quickly filter out the related information from a large number of blockchain transactions. Meanwhile, he can send it to a non-member address, and group members will find a request transaction that conforms to the format. After the group key is updated, all members update their transaction addresses and broadcast to other members with the new group key.

Blockchain-based Group Key Agreement: Member Joining

step 1: The new member sends request transactions for joining

$$M_n + 1 \xrightarrow{\quad join,\ M_n+1,\ BK_{M_n+1}=G^{K_{n+1}} mod P \quad} C = \{M_1, \ldots, M_n\}$$

step 2: Every member
- update key tree by adding new member nodes and new intermediate nodes.
- removes all keys and temporarily public keys from the leaf node related to the sponsor to the root node.

The sponsor M_s additionally
- generates the new share and computes all $[key, temporarily public key]$ pairs on the key-path.
- sends broadcast-transactions to other members which carry updated tree including only the temporarily public key.

$$CUM_n + 1 \longleftarrow \underset{BKtree}{\rule{4cm}{0pt}} M_s$$

step 3: Every member
- computes the group key using BKtree.
- updates and broadcasts new Bitcoin addresses.

Member Leaving. When a member leaves the group, the initiator is the rightmost leaf node of the subtree with the same root as the leaving member. Other members delete the leaving members from the key tree to update the key tree. The original sibling node of the leaving member replaces the parent node. The initiator updates its own key and calculates other keys on the path, and finally broadcasts a new key tree of the updated temporarily public key to other members so that all-members can calculate the new group key.

Looking at the setting in Fig. 5, if a member leaves the group, every remaining member deletes $\langle 1, 1 \rangle$ and $\langle 2, 2 \rangle$. After updating the tree, the sponsor M_5 picks a new share $K_{\langle 2,3 \rangle}$, recomputes $K_{\langle 1,1 \rangle}$, $K_{\langle 0,0 \rangle}$, $BK_{\langle 2,3 \rangle}$ and $BK_{\langle 1,1 \rangle}$. Then broadcast the updated tree. Upon receiving the broadcast message, all members compute the group key. Note that M_3 cannot compute the group key, though it knows all the temporarily public key, because its share is no longer part of the group key.

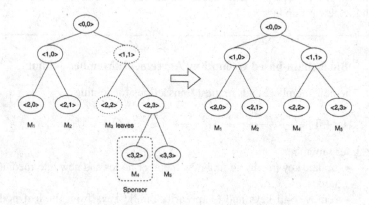

Fig. 5. A group member leaves

Blockchain-based Group Key Agreement: Member Leaving

step 1: Every member
- updates the key tree by removing the leaving member node and relevant parent node.
- removes all keys and temporarily public key from the leaf node related to the sponsor to the root node.

The sponsor M_s additionally
- generates new share and computes all $[key, temporarily public key]$ pairs on the key-path.
- sends transactions to other members which take the updated tree including the temporarily public keys.

$$M_s \xrightarrow{\quad BKtree \quad} \{M_1, \ldots, M_n\} - M_d$$

step 2: Every member
- computes the group key using the BKtree.
- updates and broadcasts new Blockchain addresses.

---

5   Security Analysis

By the BGKA protocol, the communication participants can obtain the group keys to encrypt the messages and ensure the confidentiality of the group communication. Thus how to generate and update the group keys is an important factor.

5.1   The Informal Security Analysis for the Session Key

Because of the discrete logarithm problem and the Computational Diffie-Hellman Problem, multi-party DH protocols' security has been proven [4,5,15]. If all users in the group are honest, they will get the same group keys. Each user has the ability to verify the reliability of other group members' messages by the transactions. Meanwhile, the private keys are calculated locally and not exposed to the blockchain network.

5.2   The Informal Security Analysis for the Blockchain Addresses

We analyze the security of the blockchain address by the example of the Bitcoin system. In the Bitcoin system, addresses act as the identifiers without exposing the real identity. Anyone can get new Bitcoin addresses free of charge, which consist of 27–34 alphanumeric characters. According to the rules of calculating Bitcoin's public keys and addresses, there are at most 2^{160} different addresses for one type with 256-bits private keys and RIPEMD-160 hash. There is little chance to take collision attack successfully, which means an adversary is negligible to send Bitcoin transactions through other's addresses if he knows nothing about the private keys. Moreover, the blockchain addresses update mechanism is designed to limit the number of blockchain transactions sent by the same addresses. The shorter time a Bitcoin address is used, the less likelihood of group members are exposed.

5.3   The Informal Security Analysis for Forward Secrecy and Backward Secrecy

Forward Secrecy: Any group member M_i has a private key K_i, which is used to participate in the group key agreement protocols. When the group member M_i leaves the current group, he is unable to receive any further group communication information. At the same time, after members leaving, the remaining members update their private keys and blockchain addresses. The temporarily public keys of the current group is not the same as those known by the leaving member. So leaved members cannot monitor the group's subsequent communication activity.

Backward Secrecy: New group members M_{n+1} is negligible to obtain the previous group keys to decrypt messages sent before he joins the group. In the protocol, when a new member M_{n+1} joins, some members update their private keys. So M_{n+1} cannot get previous group keys, and can only compute others' new Bitcoin addresses.

5.4   Reply Attacks

The data for the key exchange protocols and group communication in the protocol contain current timestamps, meanwhile digital signatures and blockchain system guarantee that these data and timestamp cannot be modified. The attacker has to succeed under the threshold of the time period. This is difficult because if the threshold is appropriate in the context.

5.5   Man-in-the-Middle Attacks

The security of the blockchain also directly affects the security of the man-in-the-middle attack that ultimately exchanges the key. The Diffie-Hellman key exchange is secure if there is no adversary who can actively and covertly manipulate communication information exchanged among users. The blockchain networks are peer-to-peer networks that allow users to communicate through different nodes and access the transactions. As the Bitcoin system as an example, unless the Bitcoin system with longest-chain consensus rules can be attacked by 51%-attack [9], it is difficult to change the blockchain information by other methods. Therefore, it is hard for an adversary to have the ability to change the transaction data in the ledger of the Bitcoin system. As long as all members can verify the transaction signatures, an adversary can hardly threat the security of the blockchain-based key agreement protocol unless the attacker has the ability to launch a 51% attack.

6   Conclusion and Future Work

The proposed protocols in this paper include Bitcoin address update, aiming to reduce the impact of group clustering attacks for group users' privacy. And this scheme was implemented on the real Bitcoin network without modifying the core code. Moreover, it can be used on the Ethereum, or other blockchain systems, for longer embedding space to carry information. As for the Bitcoin, the information can be transmitted in sections or slices. The scheme is compatible with different key agreement algorithms which is not exposed to the blockchain.

References

1. Bitcoin developer. https://developer.bitcoin.org/reference/transactions.html
2. Baza, M., Fouda, M.M., Nabil, M., Eldien, A.T., Mansour, H., Mahmoud, M.: Blockchain-based distributed key management approach tailored for smart grid. In: Fadlullah, Z.M., Khan Pathan, A.-S. (eds.) Combating Security Challenges in the Age of Big Data. ASTSA, pp. 237–263. Springer, Cham (2020). https://doi.org/10.1007/978-3-030-35642-2_11
3. Bui, T., Aura, T.: Key exchange with the help of a public ledger. In: Stajano, F., Anderson, J., Christianson, B., Matyáš, V. (eds.) Security Protocols 2017. LNCS, vol. 10476, pp. 123–136. Springer, Cham (2017). https://doi.org/10.1007/978-3-319-71075-4_15
4. Cheon, J.H.: Security analysis of the strong Diffie-Hellman problem. In: Vaudenay, S. (ed.) EUROCRYPT 2006. LNCS, vol. 4004, pp. 1–11. Springer, Heidelberg (2006). https://doi.org/10.1007/11761679_1
5. Boer, B.: Diffie-Hellman is as strong as discrete log for certain primes. In: Goldwasser, S. (ed.) CRYPTO 1988. LNCS, vol. 403, pp. 530–539. Springer, New York (1990). https://doi.org/10.1007/0-387-34799-2_38
6. Diffie, W., Hellman, M.: New directions in cryptography. IEEE Trans. Inf. Theory **22**(6), 644–654 (1976)
7. Han, S., Choi, R., Kim, K.: Adding authenticity into tree-based group key agreement by public ledger. In: 2019 Symposium on Cryptography and Information Security (SCIS 2019). IEICE Technical Committee on Information Security (2019)
8. Hao, F.: On robust key agreement based on public key authentication. In: Sion, R. (ed.) FC 2010. LNCS, vol. 6052, pp. 383–390. Springer, Heidelberg (2010). https://doi.org/10.1007/978-3-642-14577-3_33
9. Kroll, J.A., Davey, I.C., Felten, E.W.: The economics of bitcoin mining, or bitcoin in the presence of adversaries. In: Proceedings of WEIS, vol. 2013, p. 11 (2013)
10. Lin, I.C., Liao, T.C.: A survey of blockchain security issues and challenges. IJ Netw. Secur. **19**(5), 653–659 (2017)
11. McCorry, P., Shahandashti, S.F., Clarke, D., Hao, F.: Authenticated key exchange over bitcoin. In: Chen, L., Matsuo, S. (eds.) SSR 2015. LNCS, vol. 9497, pp. 3–20. Springer, Cham (2015). https://doi.org/10.1007/978-3-319-27152-1_1
12. Miller, V.S.: Advances in cryptology-crypto '85 proceedings. Use of elliptic curves in cryptography, pp. 417–426 (1986)
13. Nakamoto, S.: Bitcoin: A peer-to-peer electronic cash system. Technical report, Manubot (2008)
14. Steiner, M., Tsudik, G., Waidner, M.: Diffie-Hellman key distribution extended to group communication. In: Proceedings of the 3rd ACM Conference on Computer and Communications Security, pp. 31–37 (1996)
15. Steiner, M., Tsudik, G., Waidner, M.: Key agreement in dynamic peer groups. IEEE Trans. Parallel Distrib. Syst. **11**(8), 769–780 (2000)
16. Zhang, Q., et al.: Blockchain-based asymmetric group key agreement protocol for internet of vehicles. Comput. Electr. Eng. **86**, 106713 (2020)

Attacking Community Detectors: Mislead Detectors via Manipulating the Graph Structure

Kaibin Wan[1], Jiamou Liu[3], Yiwei Liu[1], Zijian Zhang[2,3]([✉]),
and Bakhadyr Khoussainov[4]

[1] School of Computer Science and Technology, Beijing Institute of Technology, Beijing, China
{kaibinwan,yiweiliu}@bit.edu.cn
[2] School of Cyberspace Science and Technology, Beijing Institute of Technology,
Beijing, China
zhangzijian@bit.edu.cn
[3] School of Computer Science, The University of Auckland, Auckland, New Zealand
jiamou.liu@auckland.ac.nz
[4] School of Computer Science and Engineering, University of Electronic Science
and Technology of China, Chengdu, China
bmk@uestc.edu.cn

Abstract. Community detection has been widely studied from many different perspectives, which include heuristic approaches in the past and graph neural network in recent years. With increasing security and privacy concerns, community detectors have been demonstrated to be vulnerable. A slight perturbation to the graph data can greatly change the detection results. In this paper, we focus on dealing with a kind of attack on one of the communities by manipulating the graph structure. We formulate this case as target community problem. The big challenge to solve this problem is the universality on different detectors. For this, we define structural information gain (SIG) to guide the manipulation and design an attack algorithm named SIGM. We compare SIGM with some recent attacks on five graph datasets. Results show that our attack is effective on misleading community detector.

Keywords: Adversarial community detection · Graph neural network · Structural entropy

1 Introduction

Real-world activities can usually be abstracted into networks, where entities are abstracted into nodes, and relationships or interactions between them are abstracted into edges. Entities naturally form communities because of their interaction. In general, a community is usually defined as a group of nodes with close internal interactions and sparse external interactions [11,21]. Analyzing communities in networks is one of the most active research directions due to its wide applications in the study of

This paper is supported by National Natural Science Foundation of China No. 62172040, No. U1836212, No. 61872041.

social structures, biological interactions, collaboration networks, etc. [5,6,20,22,32]. The main task of identifying communities is community detection. Classical approaches mainly focus on optimizing a community-quality scores [1,8,26], random walk [25,28], and graph embedding [29,30]. The methods usually follow a unsupervised learning paradigm and only concern the topological structure of a graph. Modern approaches recast community detection as a node-wise classification task. The nodes with the same label can be consider as that they are in the same community. The main difference is that traditional community detection only concerns topology information, while the node-wise classification task will concern both node attributes and topology information. The representative work is graph neural network [7,13,33], where it could be unsupervised, semi-supervised and supervised.

Recent years, graph-based community detection algorithms have been widely applied to real world such as topic classification [27], malware detection [31], finding criminal organization [9], identifying auction fraud [24] and analyzing chromosomal domains [17], and they have achieved remarkable performance in those task. However, the community detection algorithms has been proved unreliable and vulnerable against perturbation [39]. For example, the node classification algorithm will be fooled if the attackers control several fake nodes and insert or delete some edges between fake nodes and other benign nodes. Zügner et al. [39] first study this attack by slightly changing the topology structure and node feature.

With the concern about security of graph-based classification, a surge of works have been done on adversarial model [10,18,23,35,36,39]. Based on the adversary's knowledge of target model, the attack can be characterized as three threatening levels, that is, white-box attack, gray-box attack and black-box attack [4]. Specifically, the attackers able to process all information of the target model in the white-box attack, process limited knowledge in the gray-box attack, and know nothing but do limited queries in the black-box attack. In terms of the adversary's goal, there exists targeted and untargeted attack. In targeted attack, the attacker aims to let the train model misclassify a small set of nodes, while, in the untargeted attack, the attacker aims to let the train model misclassify nodes as many as possible. In terms of the attack strategy, it contains topology attack and feature attack. For topology attack, the attackers are allowed to add or remove some edges in the graph to mislead the classifier, and for feature attack, the attackers can change the features of some specified nodes [3,38].

The goal of this paper is to perform community detection attacks from the perspective of information theory. Liu et al. have introduced residual entropy to solve this problem [23]. They develop an algorithm named REM to do the non-targeted attack. However, in most cases, the attackers do not have the ability to modify the edges of all the nodes and only a few nodes' misclassification are important to the attacker but not for all the nodes. On the other hand, REM's topology attack only consider adding edges. But, in fact, deleting edges is equally important. At last, attackers generally know nothing about the targeted classifier, that is, they do not have access to the classifier's parameter or training labels. Therefore, in this paper, we focus on doing black-box and targeted attack. The attackers have the ability to add or delete edges link nodes in target community. To solve this problem has three challenges: The first is the lack of universally-agreeable definition to model the structure of targeted community, which can view as an index to guide the targeted attack. The second is the black-box problem.

There are many models to do community detection including the classical and modern methods which make it hard to pinpoint a single objective metric to cheat all the models. The third is to achieve an efficient attack with a low complexity.

In this work, we defined structural information gain (SIG) as a new metric to guide the black-box and targeted attack. By minimizing SIG, we propose a SIGM-ATTACK algorithm to cheat the classifiers to do the correct classification by adding or removing edges. Our contribution are summarized as follow:

- We define structural information gain from a view of information theory which aims to reflect the information revealed from community structure.
- We propose an effective model to mislead the node classification of the target community by minimizing SIG. We further give an efficient algorithm SIGM-ATTACK with a low compute complexity $O(|V| + |C_t|)$.
- We experimentally validate the performance of our SIG-ATTACK on 5 community detection algorithm including the classical and modern ones.

2   Related Work

Community Detection. Communities occur in many network systems from biology, computer science, politics etc. In recent years, community detection has attracted many works due to a huge amount of data and computational resource [11]. Traditional community detection algorithms aim to classify nodes in a graph into subgraphs with tight internal connections and sparse external connections based on the topology of the graph. Some of them focus on optimizing a metric, like Modularity [1,8], Spinglass [26], and structure entropy [16]. Some of them are based on random walk, for example, the idea that random walks are more likely to stay in the same community [25] and the shortest description length for a random walk [28]. Some of them are graph embedding, like spectral clustering algorithm [34], sequence-based embedding [29] and probabilistic generative model [30]. Modern algorithms recast community detection as a node-wise classification task [37]. They not only pay attention to the topology of the complex network but also the features of each node. In general, every node has a label which can be considered as its community's name. The goal of these algorithms is to predict the labels of the remaining nodes. Motivated by convolutional neural network (CNN) [15] and recurrent neural network (RNN) [12], Graph neural network (GNN) appears as a new generalization to deal with graph data [37]. Bruna et al. firstly proposed a CNN-type architecture on graphs by formulated convolution-like operations in the spectral domain [2]. After that, many work emerged along this direction [7,13,33].

Attacks on Community Detection. Many studies of successful attacks indicate that community detection algorithms are vulnerable against perturbation [39]. Chen et al. provide taxonomies for various attacks [4]. Based on the attacker's knowledge of the target community detection model, they can be divided into white-box, gray-box and black-box attack. Based on attackers' goal, there are targeted attack and untargeted attacks. As for attackers' strategy, there are topology attack, feature attack and their hybrid. Based on different manipulation methods, the attacker can perform add, remove or rewiring operation. In addition, from the perspective of the attacker, there are gradient-based and non-gradient-based algorithms. In our work, we focus on *black-box, targeted, non-gradient-based topology attack* with the add and remove manipulation. There are work on similar research with ours. Waniek et al. first came up with an algorithm named DICE to hide the target community [35]. DICE is inspired by modularity and worked by randomly deleting internal edge and adding external edge for the target community. Fionda et al. further extend the idea and propose the concept of community deception [10]. They devised two attack methods: one is based on maximizing safeness and the other is based on minimizing modularity. Later, based on GNN, Li et al. proposed an iterative attack model which learns to select the suitable candidate edges [18]. However, none of them do attack on the modern community detection algorithms. [35] and [10] only did attack on traditional detection algorithms and did not consider the graph data with features. [18] directly replaces all detection algorithms with a surrogate model and only did experiments on two data sets. In this paper, we will verify our attack algorithm on ten community detection algorithms and eight data sets. The community detection algorithms contain four optimized graph metric algorithms, two random-walk-based algorithms, two graph neural network algorithms, and heuristic algorithms. The data set also contains two forms, namely, with node features and without node features.

3   Problem Formulation

In this section, we will firstly give a general perspective of attackers' model and then give a formulation of our targeted attack.

3.1   Attacker's Model

The attacker's model includes the adversary's goal, knowledge, and abilities. We have roughly introduced it in the related work section, and below we will discuss these aspects in detail.

Attacker's Goal: In general, the attacker's goal can be divided in two categories:

- **Untargeted Attack:** In this attack, the attacker's purpose is to fool the detection algorithm so that the system has poor overall performance on the input graph data.
- **Targeted Attack:** In this attack, the attacker only focuses on a small set of nodes in the graph data and its purpose is to fool the detection algorithm to have the correct classification on those nodes.

In this paper, we consider the targeted attack on a set of nodes in the same community, since the set of nodes in different communities can be regarded as the union of sets of nodes in the same community.

Attacker's Knowledge: A complete community detection task includes datasets and the community detection algorithms on those datasets. Therefore, the background knowledge of an attacker can be summarized along two dimensions:

- **Graph Dataset:** This dimension characterized the attacker's knowledge about the dataset, including the global data, partial data, and labeled data. For graphs with features on nodes, the attacker's knowledge also includes whether they know the features of the nodes.

- **Algorithm or Classifier:** This dimension characterized the attacker's knowledge about the community detection algorithm, including algorithm settings and optimization methods. For node-wise classifier, it also includes whether there are supervision and classifier parameters, etc.

In this paper, we focus on black-box attack, that is, for the knowledge of the algorithm, the attacker knows nothing about the community detection algorithm besides a few limited queries. In addition, for the knowledge of graph dataset, the attacker knows the topological structure information and the node features of the target community.

Attacker's Capability: The capability of an attacker is reflected in the use of the attacker's knowledge. Therefore, the attacker's capabilities can be divided into three categories:

- **Modifying structure:** In this case, the attacker can make some perturbations on the topology of the graph data. Some common perturbations include adding edges, deleting edges, injecting nodes, and so on.
- **Modifying feature:** In this case, the attacker can slightly change some of the node features.
- **Modifying classifier:** In this case, the attacker has a certain ability to modify the community detection algorithm, for example, modifying the model parameters and gradient information.

In this paper, the attacker only has the ability to modify the graph structure, i.e., the attacker can insert fake edges or delete existing edges. Although the attacker knows features of some nodes, the attacker has no ability to modify these features. At the same time, we are conducting a black-box attack, where the attacker cannot perform any operations on the community detection algorithm.

3.2　A Form of Topology Attack

Generally, a social network is modelled as an undirected graph $G = (V, E)$ that includes a set of nodes V represents users and a set of edges E represents the relationship among those users. Traditionally, communities in G is characterized by high internal density and low external density. Non-overlapping communities structure in G refer to a partition $\mathcal{P} = \{C_1, C_2, \ldots, C_p\}$ of V where $p \in \mathbb{N}$ is the number of communities. Traditional community detection algorithm $\mathcal{F}$ is used to mining this partition based on the topology of G. However, in reality, each node usually has its own feature. Therefore, modern community detection algorithms take the features of nodes into consideration. For supervised tasks, nodes usually have their own labels, and the algorithm will classify nodes into communities with the same labels. For unsupervised tasks, as just mentioned, the algorithm divides the nodes into partition without labels. For convenience, in this situation, we take the real partition $\mathcal{P} = \{label_1, label_2, \ldots, label_p\}$ as their label set, i.e., we denote the label of $u \in C_j$ as $label_j$. After we get a new partition $\mathcal{P}' = \{C_1', C_2', \ldots, C_q'\}$ by unsupervised community detection algorithm, we match C_i' with C_j by solving a linear sum assignment problem to find a complete assignment of

$\mathcal{P}'$ to $\mathcal{P}$ of max $\sum_i \sum_j |C_i' \cap C_j|$ [14]. If C_i' is matched with C_j, we denote the label of $u \in C_i'$ as $label_j$.

For a graph $G = (V, E)$, the goal of the attacker is to rewire some edges such that the detection algorithm can not precisely identify members in the target community. We denote an *edge rewiring* for graph $G = (V, E)$ as

$$G \odot \{u, v\} := \begin{cases} G \oplus \{u, v\} = (V, E \cup \{u, v\}) & \{u, v\} \notin E, \\ G \ominus \{u, v\} = (V, E \setminus \{u, v\}) & \{u, v\} \in E. \end{cases}$$

Given an edge set E', for all $\{u, v\} \in E'$, iteratively execute $G \odot \{u, v\}$, we get $G' = (V, E \odot E')$.

Definition 1 (Targeted community attack problem). *Given $G = (V, E)$ with feature X and a targeted community C_t. The goal of the attacker is to find a perturbed graph $G' = (V, E \odot E')$ so that any community detection algorithm $\mathscr{F}$ can obtain minimal information about C_t without changing X, i.e.,*

$$\min M(C_t | \mathscr{F}(G')), \quad subject\ to,\ |E'| \leq \Delta,$$

where M is the function to measure the information of C_t from $\mathscr{F}(G')$ and Δ is the perturbation budget.

4   Targeted Community Attack (TCA) Based on Entropy

In this section, we will study the structure of a graph based on information theory. Assume an undirected graph $G = (V, E, X)$ is composed of vertex set V, edge set E and the feature X, where a vertex is an entity, e.g., a user or computer, an edge is the relationship among two different vertexes, and the feature X is the attribute information of V. To solute TCA problem from modifying the structure, it makes sense to study the graph structure. Generally, the set V is known in the social network. Then the edges (the relationships among vertexes V) determine the structural information of a graph. How much information does an edge have? In fact, if we have already known the degrees of all the vertices, then for an edge uv, uv happens with probability $(d_u/2|E|)(d_v/2|E|)$ since u and v are independent before they form an edge. The information associated with the edge uv in G is $\log_2[(d_u/2|E|)(d_v/2|E|)]$. We define the average information of an edge in G as the edge entropy:

$$\mathcal{H}(G) := -\frac{1}{|E|} \sum_{uv \in E} \log_2[(d_u/2|E|)(d_v/2|E|)]. \tag{1}$$

The edge entropy $\mathcal{H}(G)$ of G captures the average number of bits needed to encode a relationship in G. Since choosing u and v are independent in edge uv, the average number of bits needed to encode an edge is twice the number of bits needed to encode a vertex:

$$\mathcal{H}(G) = -\frac{1}{|E|} \sum_{uv \in E} \log_2[(d_u/2|E|)(d_v/2|E|)]$$

$$= -2 \cdot \sum_{u \in V} \frac{d_u}{2|E|} \log_2 \frac{d_u}{2|E|}. \tag{2}$$

We then define the edge entropy related to the target community C_t as the average number of bits to encode a vertex $u \in C_t$.

Definition 2. *The edge entropy related to C_t in G is*

$$\mathcal{H}(C_t|G) := -\sum_{u \in C_t} \frac{d_u}{|E|} \log_2 \frac{d_u}{2|E|}. \tag{3}$$

$\mathcal{H}(G)$ expresses the average amount of information of all edges, while $\mathcal{H}(C_t|G)$ is the part of these information that relates to community C_t. Neither $\mathcal{H}(G)$ nor $\mathcal{H}(C_t|G)$ considers the community structure. Let $\mathcal{P} = \{C_1, C_2, \ldots, C_p\}$ be the community partition of V. Then the members in G are divided into p communities $\{C_1, C_2, \ldots, C_p\}$. For the edge $uv \in E$, we have two independent steps to select an edge. The first step is identifying the community, and then the second step is selecting a member from this community. Then we have two cases: (1) $u, v \in C_j$ for some j, let ν_j be the sum degree of vertices in C_j, then we select the edge uv with probability $(d_u/\nu_j)(d_v/\nu_j)$ since we only select u and v from the vertex set C_j; (2) $uv \in C_i \times C_j$ and $i \neq j$, then we first identify C_i and C_j with probability $\nu_i/2|E|$ and $\nu_j/2|E|$, and select u and v with probability d_u/ν_i and d_v/ν_j from the corresponding part X_i and X_j. Therefore, the edge information of uv is $-\log_2[(d_u/\nu_j)(d_v/\nu_j)]$ for case (1) and $-\log_2[(\nu_i/2|E|)(\nu_j/2|E|)(d_u/\nu_j)(d_v/\nu_j)]$ for case (2), where the second information can be reduced to $-\log_2[(d_u/2|E|)(d_v/2|E|)]$. Therefore, if we know the community partition, the average information of an edge is

$$\mathcal{H}_{\mathcal{P}}(G) := \frac{1}{|E|} \{\mathcal{H}_1(G) + \mathcal{H}_2(G)\} \tag{4}$$

where

$$\mathcal{H}_1(G) = -\sum_{j=1}^{p} \sum_{uv \in E \& u,v \in X_j} \log_2[(d_u/\nu_j)(d_v/\nu_j)],$$

$$\mathcal{H}_2(G) = -\sum_{j=1}^{p} \sum_{uv \in E, u \in X_j \& v \notin X_j} \log_2[(d_u/2|E|)(d_v/2|E|)].$$

$\mathcal{H}_1(G)$ and $\mathcal{H}_2(G)$ correspond to case (1) and case (2), respectively. Simplify the equation above, we have

$$\mathcal{H}_{\mathcal{P}}(G) = \sum_{j=1}^{L} \sum_{u \in C_j} \left(-\frac{d_u^{in}}{|E|} \log_2 \frac{d_u}{\nu_j} - \frac{d_u^{out}}{|E|} \log_2 \frac{d_u}{2|E|} \right) \tag{5}$$

where d_u^{in} is the number of nodes $v \in C_j$ links u and d_u^{out} is the number of nodes $v \in V \setminus C_j$ links u.

Definition 3. *The structural entropy related to C_t in G is*

$$\mathcal{H}_{\mathcal{P}}(C_t|G) := \sum_{u \in C_t} \left(-\frac{d_u^{in}}{|E|} \log_2 \frac{d_u}{\nu_t} - \frac{d_u^{out}}{|E|} \log_2 \frac{d_u}{2|E|} \right) \tag{6}$$

and ν_t is the volume of the community C_t.

The distinction between $\mathcal{H}(C_t|G)$ and $\mathcal{H}_\mathcal{P}(C_t|G)$ is that whether the vertices in C_t know their community members. We define their difference as structural information gain revealed from community C_t:

Definition 4. *The structural information gain related to the community C_t in G is*

$$\mathcal{C}_\mathcal{P}(C_t|G) := \mathcal{H}(C_t|G) - \mathcal{H}_\mathcal{P}(C_t|G). \tag{7}$$

Let ν_t is the volume of C_t and g_t is the number of edges linked outside from C_t, then

$$\mathcal{C}_\mathcal{P}(C_t|G) = -\sum_{u \in C_t} -\frac{d_u^{in}}{|E|} \log_2 \frac{\nu_t}{2|E|}$$

$$= -\frac{\nu_t - g_t}{|E|} \log_2 \frac{\nu_t}{2|E|} \tag{8}$$

$$= -\sum_{uv \in E \& u, v \in C_t} \log_2 (\frac{\nu_t}{2|E|})^2 \tag{9}$$

The probability that an edge's endpoints happen in C_t is $(\nu_t/2|E|)^2$. Then from Eq. (9), $\mathcal{C}_\mathcal{P}(C_t|G)$ is the average information that the endpoints of an edge uv are both in C_t. It reflects the information revealed by community C_t. A high value of $\mathcal{C}_\mathcal{P}(C_t|G)$ expresses the closed connection within C_t, and a low value means the sparse connections within C_t. In particular, if there is no edge within community C_t, $\mathcal{C}_\mathcal{P}(C_t|G) = 0$. Therefore, if we say $\mathcal{H}(C_t|G)$ is the whole information of C_t in G, $\mathcal{C}_\mathcal{P}(C_t|G)$ would be the community information that community C_t takes shape because of the known members in C_t.

Lemma 1. *The maximum decrease of $\mathcal{C}_\mathcal{P}(C_t|G \oplus \{u,v\})$ happens only when the are exactly one endpoint of $\{u,v\}$ belongs to C_t. Similarly, the maximum decrease of $\mathcal{C}_\mathcal{P}(C_t|G \ominus \{u,v\})$ happens only when both u and v belong to C_t.*

Proof. Denote $\mathcal{C}_\mathcal{P}(C_t|G \odot \{u,v\}) = g(u,v)$ for the rewire edge $\{u,v\}$. Let $k = 1$ if $\odot = \oplus$, $k = -1$ if $\odot = \ominus$; and $|E| = m$. Then if $u_1, v_1, u_2 \in C_t$, $v_2, u_3, v_3 \notin C_t$, from (8), we have

$$\begin{cases} g(u_1, v_1) = -\frac{\nu_t - g_t + 2k}{2m+2k} \log_2 \frac{\nu_t + 2k}{2m+2k}, \\ g(u_2, v_2) = -\frac{\nu_t - g_t}{2m+2k} \log_2 \frac{\nu_t + k}{2m+2k}, \\ g(u_3, v_3) = -\frac{\nu_t - g_t}{2m+2k} \log_2 \frac{\nu_t}{2m+2k}. \end{cases}$$

Let $\gamma = -1/(2m+2k)$, then

$$\begin{cases} g(u_2, v_2) - g(u_3, v_3) = \gamma(\nu_t - g_t) \log_2 \frac{\nu_t + k}{\nu_t} \\ g(u_3, v_3) - g(u_1, v_1) = \gamma \log_2 (\frac{\nu_t}{\nu_t + 2k})^{\nu_t - g_t} (\frac{2m+2k}{\nu_t + 2k})^{2k} \end{cases}$$

Since $(1 + 1/x)^x$ is monotonically increasing, $\lim_{x \to +\infty}(1 + 1/x)^x = e$ and $\frac{2m+2k}{\nu_t + 2k} \geq \sqrt{e}$ where e is natural logarithm, we have $g(u_2, v_2) \leq g(u_3, v_3) \leq g(u_1, v_1)$ if $k = 1$ and $g(u_1, v_1) \leq g(u_3, v_3) \leq g(u_2, v_2)$ if $k = -1$.

Remark 1. Lemma 1 shows the general principle for hiding a community is adding external and deleting internal (AEDI).

Since the value of $\mathcal{C}_{\mathcal{P}}(C_t|G)$ is related to the size of G, then a natural definition of the normalized structural information gain is:

$$\rho_t(G) := \mathcal{C}_{\mathcal{P}}(C_t|G)/\mathcal{H}(C_t|G). \tag{10}$$

So, if we want to attack a community C_t, we would like to minimize $\rho_t(G)$. Denote a structural information gain minimization (SIGM) attack as an algorithm that outputs a rewiring edge e such that $\rho_t(G \odot e)$ is minimized. A crude implementation of a SIGM attack according for the principle AEDI to examine each potential edge e that connects external for $\rho_t(G \oplus e)$ and disconnect internal $\rho_t(G \ominus e)$. This implementation runs in $O(|C_t||V|)$ time since it takes $|C_t|(|V| - |C_t|)$ for adding and $|C_t|^2$ for deleting, but it is still inapplicable for large graphs. We instead present an $O(\log|V| + |C_t|)$-implementation in Algorithm 1 according to the following Lemmas.

Lemma 2. *For any edge $\{u, v\} \notin E$, $u \in C_t$ and $v \notin C_t$ where C_t is the target community. The maximum decrease of $\rho_t(G \oplus \{u, v\})$ happens only when d_u is minimum.*

Proof. For any $u_1, u_2 \in C_t$, $v \notin C_t$, we have $\mathcal{C}_{\mathcal{P}}(C_t|G \oplus \{u_1, v\}) = \mathcal{C}_{\mathcal{P}}(C_t|G \oplus \{u_2, v\})$ from (8). Then, assume $d_{u_1} < d_{u_2}$, from (10), we only need to prove $\mathcal{H}(C_t|G \oplus \{u_1, v\}) > \mathcal{H}(C_t|G \oplus \{u_2, v\})$. Define the function $F: \mathbb{R} \to \mathbb{R}$ by $F(x) = (x + 1)\log_2(x + 1) - x\log_2(x)$. The function F is *monotonically increasing*, as $F'(x) = \log_2(x + 1) - \log_2(x) > 0$. Then, we finish the proof since $\mathcal{H}(C_t|G \oplus \{u_1, v\}) - \mathcal{H}(C_t|G \oplus \{u_2, v\}) = \frac{1}{2(|E|+1)}(F(d_{u_2}) - F(d_{u_1})) > 0$.

For $\{x, y\} \in E$, we call $\{x, y\} \in C_t \times C_t$ is critical if d_y is maximum among all x's neighbors in C_t.

Lemma 3. *There exists a critical edge $\{u, v\}$ such that $\rho_t(G \ominus \{u, v\})$ is minimum.*

Proof. Assume $\{u, v\}$ is the best edge such that $\rho_X(G \ominus \{u, v\})$ is minimum among all edges in $C_t \times C_t$. If $\{u, v\}$ is not a critical edge, then either u or v is not the other one's neighbor with the maximum degree. Without loss of generality, we assume v is not u's neighbor with the maximum degree and w is. Define $F(x)$ as described in Lemma 2. Since the function F is *monotonically increasing* for $x > 0$, then $\mathcal{H}(C_t|G \ominus \{u, w\}) - \mathcal{H}(C_t|G \ominus \{u, v\}) = \frac{1}{2(|E|-1)}(F(d_w - 1) - F(d_v - 1)) > 0$. We finish the proof since $\mathcal{C}_{\mathcal{P}}(C_t|G \ominus \{u, v\}) = \mathcal{C}^{\mathcal{P}}(C_t|G \ominus \{u, w\})$ and (10).

Theorem 1. *Algorithm 1 implements SIGM in $O(\log|V| + |C_t|)$.*

Proof. For adding edge, the Algorithm 1 will take $O(1)$ operations to find minimum degree and $O(\log|V|)$ operations to update the degree sequence $SeqV$. For deleting edge, Algorithm 1 will take $O(|C_t|)$ operations to go over all critical edges and at most $O(|C_t|)$ operations to update the critical edges $CriC$.

Algorithm 1. An efficient SIGM attack

Input: Graph $G = (V, E)$, $\mathcal{P} = \{C_1, C_2, \ldots, C_p\}$, $1 \leq t \leq p$
Output: A non-edge $\{u^*, v^*\}$
1: Precalculate the degree sequence $SeqV$ from small to large for V and the critical edge set $CriC$ for C_t
2: Choose $u \in C_t$ from $SeqV$ s.t. d_u is minimum
3: Randomly choose $v \notin C_t$ from $SeqV$ limited in $V \backslash C_t$ s.t. $\{u, v\} \notin E$ and d_v is minimum
4: Go over all critical edges in $CriC$ to select an edge $\{x, y\}$ s.t. $\rho_t(G \ominus \{x, y\})$ is minimum
5: **if** $\rho_t(G \oplus \{u, v\}) \leq \rho_t(G \ominus \{x, y\})$ **then**
6:     Set $u^* \leftarrow u$, $v^* \leftarrow v$
7: **else**
8:     Set $u^* \leftarrow x$, $v^* \leftarrow y$
9: **end if**
10: Update the sequence $SeqV$ and the edge set $CriC$
11: **return** $\{u^*, v^*\}$

---

5   Experiments

In this section, we will evaluate the performance of our algorithm SIGM on five real-world datasets where three datasets contain the node features and the others do not contain node features. In our experimental settings, we choose both traditional and modern community detection algorithms as the targets of the attack, and three attack algorithms as the benchmark. Finally, we use experimental results to verify that our algorithm can achieve good performance on both traditional and modern community detection algorithms.

Table 1. Specifics of the datasets, where C_t is the target community and $E(C_t)$ is the edge set in C_t.

Dataset	V	E	Targeted community	
			$(|C_1|, |E_1|)$	$(|C_2|, |E_2|)$
Email	1133	5451	(214, 784)	(303, 1053)
DBLP	317080	1049866	(746, 1990)	(463, 1262)
Amazon	334863	925872	(351, 810)	(399, 1139)
Cora	2708	5429	(818, 1175)	(180, 253)
Citeseer	3312	4732	(668, 1041)	(701, 1016)

5.1   Data

We will evaluate the performance of our algorithm over two types of datasets:

- one type is the real social network without node features, including the email communication network between members of the Univeristy Rovira i Virgili (**Email**[1]),

---

[1] https://deim.urv.cat/~alexandre.arenas/data/welcome.htm.

the co-authorship network in DBLP (**DBLP**[2]) and the co-purchased network in Amazon (**Ama**[2]).
- the other type is the real social network with node features, including three citation networks of 2708 and 3312 scientific publications respectively (**Cora**[3] and Citeseer[3]).

Table 1 gives an overview of the datasets. In each dataset, we choose two communities as our target community. In our experiments, we will rewire a certain ratio edges of $E(C_t)$, where $E(C_t)$ is the edge set within the target community C_t. It should be noted that because the data of **DBLP** and **Amazon** is too large, here we only extracted 3095 nodes of data DBLP and 10328 nodes of data Amazon.

5.2   Benchmark, Community Detectors and Metrics

Benchmark. Given a social network $G = (V, E)$ and the target community C_t, we use the following attack algorithms as our benchmark:

- Random Attack (**RND**), which follows the algorithms RND in [39]. At each rewiring step, randomly sample a node v in V. If v is not directly connected to any node in C_t, we randomly choose a node u in in C_t and add an edge between u and v; otherwise we delete one of the directly connected edge between v and C_t.
- **DICE**, which follows the heuristic attack idea that **D**isconnect **I**nternally and **C**onnect **E**xternally in [35]. It works via the following steps given a budget Δ: (1) randomly delete $\Delta_d \leq \Delta$ edges from within the community C_t; and (2) randomly insert $\Delta - \Delta_d$ edges between C_t and the rest nodes $V \backslash C_t$.
- Modularity Based Attack (**MBA**) [10], which weaken the target community by minimizing modularity. At each rewiring step, the algorithm will add or delete an edge that links to C_t and has the minimal modularity.

Community Detectors. We consider five well-known community detection algorithms as our object to verify our attack performance. The detectors contain both traditional and modern community detection algorithms.

(1) Louvain [1]: a heuristic multi-level modularity maximizing algorithm.
(2) InfoMap [28]: an optimization algorithm by providing the shortest description length for a random walk.
(3) EdMot [19]: an Edge enhancement approach for Motif-aware community detection.
(4) GCN [13]: a scalable approach that is based on an efficient variant of convolutional neural networks.
(5) GAT [33]: a novel neural network architectures following a self-attention strategy to compute the hidden representations of each node by attending over its neighbors in the graph.

---

[2] http://snap.stanford.edu/data/.
[3] https://paperswithcode.com/datasets?mod=graphs.

Metrics. We introduce two measures to quantify the degree of attack. Given a network $G = (V, E)$ and the target community C_t, the goal is let C_t escape detection from community detector $\mathscr{F}$, which means that we cannot refer C_t from $\mathscr{F}(G') = \mathcal{P}'$, where G' is the perturbed graph after attack. Therefore, how to measure the extent that we can refer C_t from $\mathcal{P}'$ is the key to evaluate the effect of an attack. Here we introduce information entropy to give an explainable definition. Let $\mathcal{P}' = \{C_1', C_2', \dots, C_q'\}$.

$$H(C_t) = -\frac{|C_t|}{|V|} \log \frac{|C_t|}{|V|},$$

$$H(C_t|\mathcal{P}') = -\sum_{j=1}^{q} \frac{|C_t \cap C_j'|}{|V|} \log \frac{|C_t \cap C_j'|/|V|}{|C_j'|/|V|}.$$

$H(C_t)$ is the amount of uncertain information to encode the target community C_t in G. $H(C_t|\mathcal{P}')$ is the residual uncertain information if we have the partition $\mathcal{P}'$. Thus, normalized mutual information for C_t is defined as $I(C_t, \mathcal{P}') = (H(C_t) - H(C_t|\mathcal{P}'))/H(C_t)$. Of course, a low $I(X, \mathcal{P})$ means a good attack.

On the other hand, we consider a measure widely used in machine learning, F1-score. Let C_t is the target community, the F1 score for C_t is defined as:

$$F_1 = \frac{2 \times \mathcal{R}(C_t, C_s') \times \mathcal{P}(C_t, C_s')}{\mathcal{R}(C_t, C_s') + \mathcal{P}(C_t, C_s')}$$

where

$$\mathcal{R}(C_t, C_s') = \frac{|C_t \cap C_s'|}{|C_t|},$$

$$\mathcal{P}(C_t, C_s') = \frac{|C_t \cap C_s'|}{|C_s'|},$$

where C_s' has the same label with C_t. Similarly, the smaller the value of F1, the better the attack effect.

5.3 Experimental Settings and Results

Experimental Settings. We compare SIGM with three other attack algorithms, including RND, DICE and MBA. We conduct experiments on the four algorithms. The setup and process of the experiment are described as follows: (1) Randomly choose a community C_t as the target community from the ground truth network $G = (V, E)$; (2) Calculate a certain ratio edges of $|E(C_t)|$ by applying an attack on the initial network G, and output the edge set E'; (3) Calculate the new community partition $\mathcal{P}'$ by applying community detector $\mathscr{F}$ on the perturbed network $G \odot E'$, i.e., $\mathcal{P}' = \mathscr{F}(G \odot E')$; (4) Calculate the metrics $\{I, F1\}$ for the target community C_t based on the new community partition $\mathcal{P}'$.

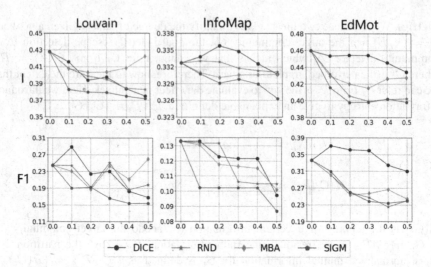

Fig. 1. The effect after applying attack RND, MBA, DICE and SIGM for a target community of dataset DBLP.

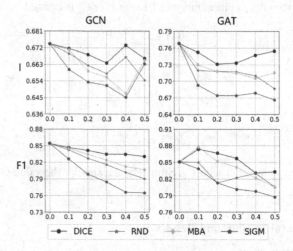

Fig. 2. The effect after applying attack RND, MBA, DICE and SIGM for a community of dataset Cora.

Experimental Results. We examine the performance of the four attacks over five datasets by modifying a certain ratio edges of $E(C_t)$. In Table 2, the ratio is 30%. Table 2 compares the attack effect score $I, F1$ with the other three attacks. Clearly, SIGM performs better than RND, DICE and MBA in most scenarios. In Fig. 1 and Fig. 2, we show the detailed trend of $I, \mathscr{F}1$ scores with the ratio of budget edges for the data DBLP and Cora. The indicators $\{I, F1\}$, which used to evaluate the effectiveness of detection algorithm, decrease significantly as the cost of perturbing the graph increasing. Obviously, all attacks are effective, but the performance is still different.

Table 2. The value of I and $F1$ for different attacks on 5 kinds of community detectors after modifying 30% edges of $E(C_t)$.

Data	Detector	NMI (I)				F1-score (F1)			
		RND	DICE	MBA	SIGM	RND	DICE	MBA	SIGM
Email	Louvain	0.527	0.542	0.516	**0.501**	0.563	0.522	0.517	**0.449**
		0.445	0.447	0.465	**0.435**	0.578	0.549	0.574	**0.440**
	InfoMap	0.351	0.353	0.352	**0.338**	0.273	0.268	0.267	**0.233**
		0.276	0.277	0.277	**0.274**	0.170	0.187	**0.169**	0.186
	EdMot	0.476	0.495	0.488	**0.457**	0.447	0.472	0.447	**0.416**
		0.391	0.392	0.404	**0.386**	0.305	0.309	0.369	**0.297**
DBLP	Louvain	0.326	0.337	0.341	**0.318**	**0.278**	0.290	0.305	0.306
		0.383	0.390	0.413	**0.370**	0.193	0.209	0.208	**0.183**
	InfoMap	0.258	0.258	0.257	**0.254**	0.112	0.111	**0.105**	0.118
		0.333	0.330	0.330	**0.326**	0.118	0.109	0.120	**0.087**
	EdMot	0.339	0.369	0.360	**0.332**	0.286	0.345	0.324	**0.257**
		0.403	0.440	0.427	**0.403**	**0.250**	0.330	0.311	0.253
Amazon	Louvain	0.617	0.715	0.630	**0.559**	0.330	0.432	0.351	**0.313**
		0.695	0.776	0.721	**0.601**	0.674	0.735	0.556	**0.463**
	InfoMap	0.539	0.548	0.540	**0.529**	0.296	0.324	0.303	**0.27**
		0.607	0.664	0.623	**0.568**	0.676	0.763	0.686	**0.617**
	EdMot	0.710	0.910	0.736	**0.709**	0.727	0.951	**0.681**	0.739
		0.775	0.910	0.824	**0.710**	0.873	0.962	0.773	**0.766**
Cora	GCN	0.666	0.662	**0.651**	0.656	0.813	0.837	0.823	**0.783**
		0.698	0.721	0.710	**0.680**	0.723	0.771	0.694	**0.692**
	GAT	0.701	0.730	0.708	**0.693**	0.835	0.856	0.838	**0.792**
		0.696	0.771	0.732	**0.687**	**0.588**	0.804	0.664	0.599
Citeseer	GCN	0.682	0.688	0.679	**0.667**	0.727	0.754	0.728	**0.711**
		0.656	0.654	0.655	**0.641**	0.773	0.792	0.773	**0.760**
	GAT	0.667	0.669	**0.649**	0.657	0.716	0.749	0.716	**0.685**
		0.646	0.650	0.657	**0.646**	0.751	0.789	0.743	**0.736**

SIGM performs better than RND, DICE and MBA in most of sampling point and much more stable than other three benchmarks. Thus the result validates SIGM's effectiveness in attacking the target community.

Although all the four attacks are effective, there are still fluctuations in the downward trend of indicators $I, F1$. This can be explained in two perspectives. On the one hand, the fluctuation may be caused by the attack algorithm. For example, the DICE is a heuristic algorithm, which controls the proportion of adding and deleting operations equals 0.5 on average. But this ratio is affected by the community structure, so some of the perturbations taken by DICE are invalid or even counterproductive. On the other hand, the robustness of the community detectors will also cause such fluctuations. In general, the graph embedding algorithms are more robust than traditional community detectors. That's why the attacks over EdMot, GCN and GAT are more stable than Louvain and InfoMap in Fig. 1.

6 Conclusion

In this paper, we introduce the target community attack problem, utilize community based structural information to the this problem, and propose a structural information gain minimization (SIGM) algorithm. We optimize SIGM to make it more efficient. Experiments in the real world network show that our algorithm SIGM performs better than RND, DICE and MBA in most of attack scenarios. Some future works include (1) attacking some important nodes, e.g., influential nodes, hierarchies, etc. (2) attacking the communities in weighted and directed graphs; (3) exploring some new metric as evaluation score (4) Combining the information with differential privacy on graphs.

References

1. Blondel, V.D., Guillaume, J.L., Lambiotte, R., Lefebvre, E.: Fast unfolding of communities in large networks. J. Stat. Mech. **2008**(10), P10008 (2008)
2. Bruna, J., Zaremba, W., Szlam, A., LeCun, Y.: Spectral networks and locally connected networks on graphs. arXiv preprint arXiv:1312.6203 (2013)
3. Cai, Y., Zheng, H., Liu, J., Yan, B., Su, H., Liu, Y.: Balancing the pain and gain of hobnobbing: utility-based network building over atributed social networks. In: Proceedings of the 17th International Conference on Autonomous Agents and MultiAgent Systems, pp. 193–201 (2018)
4. Chen, L., et al.: A survey of adversarial learning on graphs. arXiv preprint arXiv:2003.05730 (2020)
5. Chen, Q., Su, H., Liu, J., Yan, B., Zheng, H., Zhao, H.: In pursuit of social capital: upgrading social circle through edge rewiring. In: Shao, J., Yiu, M.L., Toyoda, M., Zhang, D., Wang, W., Cui, B. (eds.) APWeb-WAIM 2019. LNCS, vol. 11641, pp. 207–222. Springer, Cham (2019). https://doi.org/10.1007/978-3-030-26072-9_15
6. Chen, Y., Liu, J.: Distributed community detection over blockchain networks based on structural entropy. In: Proceedings of the 2019 ACM International Symposium on Blockchain and Secure Critical Infrastructure, pp. 3–12 (2019)
7. Chen, Z., Li, X., Bruna, J.: Supervised community detection with line graph neural networks. arXiv preprint arXiv:1705.08415 (2017)
8. Clauset, A., Newman, M.E., Moore, C.: Finding community structure in very large networks. Phys. Rev. E **70**(6), 066111 (2004)
9. Ferrara, E., De Meo, P., Catanese, S., Fiumara, G.: Detecting criminal organizations in mobile phone networks. Expert Syst. Appl. **41**(13), 5733–5750 (2014)
10. Fionda, V., Pirro, G.: Community deception or: how to stop fearing community detection algorithms. IEEE Trans. Knowl. Data Eng. **30**(4), 660–673 (2017)
11. Fortunato, S.: Community detection in graphs. Phys. Rep. **486**(3–5), 75–174 (2010)
12. Hochreiter, S., Schmidhuber, J.: Long short-term memory. Neural Comput. **9**(8), 1735–1780 (1997)

13. Kipf, T.N., Welling, M.: Semi-supervised classification with graph convolutional networks. arXiv preprint arXiv:1609.02907 (2016)

14. Kuhn, H.W.: The hungarian method for the assignment problem. Naval Res. Logist. Q. **2**(1–2), 83–97 (1955)

15. LeCun, Y., Bengio, Y., et al.: Convolutional networks for images, speech, and time series. Handb. Brain Theory Neural Netw. **3361**(10), 1995 (1995)

16. Li, A., Li, J., Pan, Y.: Discovering natural communities in networks. Phys. A **436**, 878–896 (2015)

17. Li, A., et al.: Decoding topologically associating domains with ultra-low resolution hi-c data by graph structural entropy. Nat. Commun. **9**(1), 3265 (2018)

18. Li, J., Zhang, H., Han, Z., Rong, Y., Cheng, H., Huang, J.: Adversarial attack on community detection by hiding individuals. In: Proceedings of The Web Conference 2020, pp. 917–927 (2020)

19. Li, P.Z., Huang, L., Wang, C.D., Lai, J.H.: Edmot: an edge enhancement approach for motif-aware community detection. In: Proceedings of the 25th ACM SIGKDD International Conference on Knowledge Discovery & Data Mining, pp. 479–487 (2019)

20. Liu, J., Minnes, M.: Deciding the isomorphism problem in classes of unary automatic structures. Theoret. Comput. Sci. **412**(18), 1705–1717 (2011)

21. Liu, J., Wei, Z.: Community detection based on graph dynamical systems with asynchronous runs. In: 2014 Second International Symposium on Computing and Networking, pp. 463–469. IEEE (2014)

22. Liu, Y., et al.: From local to global norm emergence: Dissolving self-reinforcing substructures with incremental social instruments. In: International Conference on Machine Learning, pp. 6871–6881. PMLR (2021)

23. Liu, Y., Liu, J., Zhang, Z., Zhu, L., Li, A.: Rem: from structural entropy to community structure deception. In: Advances in Neural Information Processing Systems, pp. 12938–12948 (2019)

24. Pandit, S., Chau, D.H., Wang, S., Faloutsos, C.: Netprobe: a fast and scalable system for fraud detection in online auction networks. In: Proceedings of the 16th International Conference on World Wide Web, pp. 201–210 (2007)

25. Pons, P., Latapy, M.: Computing communities in large networks using random walks. In: Yolum, I., Güngör, T., Gürgen, F., Özturan, C. (eds.) ISCIS 2005. LNCS, vol. 3733, pp. 284–293. Springer, Heidelberg (2005). https://doi.org/10.1007/11569596_31

26. Reichardt, J., Bornholdt, S.: Statistical mechanics of community detection. Phys. Rev. E **74**(1), 016110 (2006)

27. Revelle, M., Domeniconi, C., Sweeney, M., Johri, A.: Finding community topics and membership in graphs. In: Appice, A., Rodrigues, P.P., Santos Costa, V., Gama, J., Jorge, A., Soares, C. (eds.) ECML PKDD 2015. LNCS (LNAI), vol. 9285, pp. 625–640. Springer, Cham (2015). https://doi.org/10.1007/978-3-319-23525-7_38

28. Rosvall, M., Bergstrom, C.T.: Maps of random walks on complex networks reveal community structure. Proc. Natl. Acad. Sci. **105**(4), 1118–1123 (2008)

29. Rozemberczki, B., Davies, R., Sarkar, R., Sutton, C.: Gemsec: graph embedding with self clustering. In: Proceedings of the 2019 IEEE/ACM International Conference on Advances in Social Networks Analysis and Mining, pp. 65–72 (2019)

30. Sun, F.Y., Qu, M., Hoffmann, J., Huang, C.W., Tang, J.: vgraph: a generative model for joint community detection and node representation learning. In: Advances in Neural Information Processing Systems, pp. 514–524 (2019)

31. Tamersoy, A., Roundy, K., Chau, D.H.: Guilt by association: large scale malware detection by mining file-relation graphs. In: Proceedings of the 20th ACM SIGKDD International Conference on Knowledge Discovery and Data Mining, pp. 1524–1533 (2014)

32. van Laarhoven, T., Marchiori, E.: Robust community detection methods with resolution parameter for complex detection in protein protein interaction networks. In: Shibuya, T., Kashima, H., Sese, J., Ahmad, S. (eds.) PRIB 2012. LNCS, vol. 7632, pp. 1–13. Springer, Heidelberg (2012). https://doi.org/10.1007/978-3-642-34123-6_1

33. Veličković, P., Cucurull, G., Casanova, A., Romero, A., Lio, P., Bengio, Y.: Graph attention networks. arXiv preprint arXiv:1710.10903 (2017)

34. Von Luxburg, U.: A tutorial on spectral clustering. Stat. Comput. **17**(4), 395–416 (2007)

35. Waniek, M., Michalak, T.P., Wooldridge, M.J., Rahwan, T.: Hiding individuals and communities in a social network. Nat. Hum. Behav. **2**(2), 139–147 (2018)

36. Wu, H., Wang, C., Tyshetskiy, Y., Docherty, A., Lu, K., Zhu, L.: Adversarial examples on graph data: Deep insights into attack and defense. arXiv preprint arXiv:1903.01610 (2019)

37. Wu, Z., Pan, S., Chen, F., Long, G., Zhang, C., Philip, S.Y.: A comprehensive survey on graph neural networks. IEEE Trans. Neural Netw. Learn. Syst. **32**(1), 4–24 (2021)

38. Yan, B., Liu, Y., Liu, J., Cai, Y., Su, H., Zheng, H.: From the periphery to the center: information brokerage in an evolving network. In: Proceedings of the 27th International Joint Conference on Artificial Intelligence, pp. 3912–3918 (2018)

39. Zügner, D., Akbarnejad, A., Günnemann, S.: Adversarial attacks on neural networks for graph data. In: Proceedings of the 24th ACM SIGKDD International Conference on Knowledge Discovery & Data Mining, pp. 2847–2856 (2018)

ResNet-Like CNN Architecture and Saliency Map for Human Activity Recognition

Zixuan Yan[1](✉), Rabih Younes[2], and Jason Forsyth[3]

[1] Nanjing University, Nanjing, China
171180578@smail.nju.edu.cn
[2] Duke University, Durham, USA
[3] James Madison University, Harrisonburg, USA

Abstract. Human activity recognition (HAR) has been adopting deep learning to substitute well-established analysis techniques that rely on hand-crafted feature extraction and classication techniques. However, the architecture of convolutional neural network (CNN) models used in HAR tasks still mostly uses VGG-like models while more and more novel architectures keep emerging. In this work, we present a novel approach to HAR by incorporating elements of residual learning in our ResNet-like CNN model to improve existing approaches by reducing the computational complexity of the recognition task without sacrificing accuracy. Specifically, we design our ResNet-like CNN based on residual learning and achieve nearly 1% better accuracy than the state-of-the-art, with over 10 times parameter reduction. At the same time, we adopt the Saliency Map method to visualize the importance of every input channel. This enables us to conduct further work such as dimension reduction to improve computational efficiency or finding the optimal sensor node(s) position(s).

Keywords: Human activity recognition (HAR) · Convolutional neural network (CNN) · ResNet · Saliency map

1 Introduction

Human activity recognition (HAR) has recently been a research hot spot, attracting not only crowds of researchers but also plenty of funds. HAR methodologies have gotten very competent at recognizing human activities directly from raw sensor signals, which has wide applications including home behavior analysis [23], ubiquitous computing [7], health monitoring [18], etc. There are mainly two types of HAR [2]: video-based and sensor-based. We will focus on sensor-based here because of he simplicity of one-dimensional time series data and the privacy concerns it addresses.

There are mainly two types of HAR [3]: video-based and sensor-based. Video-based HAR analyzes videos of humans performing activities in front of a camera. It conforms to our intuition for recognizing human activities but suffers

S. Deng et al. (Eds.): MobiCASE 2021, LNICST 434, pp. 129–143, 2022.
https://doi.org/10.1007/978-3-030-99203-3_9

from many problems, like the complexity to process high-dimensional data, the reliance on environmental illumination, and the need for fixing the position of camera. At the same time, sensor-based HAR can process data from various sensors, such as accelerometer, gyroscope, magnetometer, Bluetooth, and other sensors. Although it requires users to wear some kind of special equipment, the simplicity of 1-dimensional time series data and the privacy concerns it addresses make it popular. There are also works on using mobile phones or smart watches as sensors, which makes it even more convenient. Therefore, in this paper, we will focus on sensor-based HAR.

In general, HAR can be treated as a typical pattern recognition problem where machine learning is very effective [2]. Conventional HAR methods adopt machine learning algorithms such as decision tree, support vector machine (SVM), naive Bayes and hidden Markov models as classifiers. However, a main problem is the heavy reliance on hand-crafted feature extraction which is constrained to the knowledge of the practitioner. Furthermore, the learnt features are always shallow and unable to generalize, which means there is no universal solution to every dataset. Due to these limitations, traditional HAR methods are restricted both in accuracy and generalization ability.

Recent years have witnessed the rise and rapid development of deep learning [13], which have achieved unparalleled performance in computer vision [12], natural language processing [1] and speech processing [9]. As a representation learning method, it can automatically learn deep features which are most useful for classification without any hand-crafted preprocessing. This advancement improves over traditional methods where the hand-crafted features are required. In [24], authors report about the existing works and future directions at the intersection of deep learning and HAR.

One of the most prominent deep learning methods are convolutional neural networks (CNN). The models are attractive in their ability to exploit spatial information inside datasets and were first used to classify images. Extending this ability to HAR, these approaches can exploit the time correlation between adjacent points in one-dimensional (1D) time series data [4,6,17,22,26,27]. However, while CNN structures in the computer vision field keep evolving, from AlexNet [12] to VGGnet [20], Inception [21], ResNet [8], DenseNet [11], MobileNet [10], and other advanced models with better performance and efficiency, the main structure of CNN in HAR field has been stuck in VGG-like model. Therefore, it is necessary to explore the possibility of applying the advancement of structures from visual field to HAR tasks.

Among diverse novel CNN structures, ResNet is one of the most commonly used and is highest performing. It won the first place of ILSVRC-2015 and was awarded the best paper of CVPR in 2016 [8] and was followed by many variants. It is serving as the main structure of many visual tasks like image classification, object recognition, semantic segmentation and so on. Although it is originally designed for images, the core idea - residual learning can be easily transplanted into one-dimensional CNN designing. In this work, we have developed a novel structure based on the same idea of ResNet for HAR. We have tested it on mainstream dataset OPPORTUNITY [3] and achieved nearly 1% better in accuracy than even the best networks to our knowledge, with over 10 times parameter reduction.

Without architecture, another essential question is that where we should put the sensor to recognize the human activity better. We creatively transplant a method called Saliency Map [19] to directly visualize the importance of every channel to the final result. Saliency Map comes from image classification field and is used to visualize which part inside the image contributes most to the classification result. The same method used here can help us find out the most important sensor without training many times or trying different combinations.

In summary, the contributions of this work are as follows:

- We put forward a novel ResNet-like CNN structure for HAR tasks with improved performance.
- The network we designed has significantly fewer parameters which is capable for more efficient computing.
- We use Saliency Map to directly visualize the importance of every input channel.

The rest of the paper is organized as follows. We discuss related work in Sect. 2. The details of our three contributions are presented in Sect. 3 (ResNet-like structure) and Sect. 4 (Saliency Map usage). The conducted experiments and results are discussed in Sect. 5. Section 6 concludes the paper and lays out potential future work.

2   Related Work

In this section, we discuss related works and contrast them with ours. Section 2.1 discusses previous works which also apply CNNs for HAR and their flaws. Section 2.2 introduces the origination of ResNet and how this residual learning idea influences our work. Section 2.3 introduces the application of Saliency Map in Computer Vision field and how it can be converted into HAR.

2.1   CNNs for HAR

As presented before, CNN has become a wide-spread tool for HAR in recent years. To our knowledge, [27] was the first work using CNN to process time series data. It treated every channel like RGB of an image but did the convolution and pooling separately, which may be considered unreasonable today. This mistake is corrected in [26], which proposed to share weights in 1D multi-channel convolution. Along with this basis, [4] did some experiments to find the optimal kernel size for HAR data. [6] did a comprehensive comparison of deep learning models for HAR, including DNN, CNN, RNN and hybrid models. Some very recent work still follows the pattern, with the changing from common filters to Lego filters [22], improving the computational efficiency for mobile applications. However, all these networks share the same main structure, only varying in number of layers or kernels. It is necessary to explore novel architectures, like employing skip connections, which is essential in state-of-the-art CNN network designing. It is worth noting that there are some works using CNN+LSTM architectures [15,25], which have higher accuracy than our architecture. However, since CNN part and LSTM part are independent to each other, the simple structure of CNN can be easily replaced with our version and it should achieve better results.

2.2   ResNet

ResNet originated from [8] and have become one of the most wide-spread architectures for deep learning networks. The core idea is residual learning, which uses shortcut connections to ease learning complexity and strengthen gradient flow. However, the original network is for 2D pictures and cannot be directly used in HAR, so we followed the core idea of residual learning and developed our new architecture for 1D time series data. Our new architecture is based on Res Block which is designed according to residual learning concept.

2.3   Saliency Map

Saliency Map [19] comes from Image Classification field and is put forward to answer the question that which part of the picture contributes most to the final classification result. There is a similar question in HAR field that which sensor is most useful or where is the optimal position of sensor to achieve best performance with fewest sensors. Therefore, we developed a 1D version of Saliency Map to visualize the importance of every input channel, which could be used for dimensionality reduction further.

3   ResNet-Like Structure

This section has a detailed description of the basic idea of residual learning and our novel network which employed similar residual learning idea. The concept of residual learning is discussed in Sect. 3.1 and the network architecture in Sect. 3.2.

3.1   Residual Learning

Our architecture shares the same basic idea with ResNet – residual learning. According to the CNN network designing principles, the architecture of a network should be based on stacking of similar blocks, in order to simplify parameter tuning and prevent from overfitting specific dataset and leading to low generalization ability. Therefore, we will explain our network design and theory behind through blocks.

The mathematical model of Residual Blocks can be shown in one line of formula:

$$y_l = F(x_l) + x_l \tag{1}$$

Here y_l denotes the output feature to the l-th residual block and x_l is the input. $F(\cdot)$ denotes residual function and is always stacks of convolutional layers. Instead of directly learning the mapping $H(x)$ from input to output in traditional CNN models, the convolutional part of residual block learns $F(x) = H(x) - x$. It can be seen as a shortcut connection from input to output.

The advantages of introducing shortcut connection can be understood in three perspectives.

First, the complexity of learning is reduced, especially when the features generated by current layer is fine-tuning of last layer's, which happens mostly in deeper networks. Take identity mapping $y = x$ for example. In traditional CNN networks, you must precisely adjust the weights to achieve $H(x) = x$. While in residual blocks, the only thing you need to do is setting all weights to zero. It means $F(x) = 0$ and $H(x) = x$.

Second, it strengthens the gradient flow. One of the most serious difficulty to train very deep CNNs is that gradient may vanish or explode during flowing from deep layers to shallow ones. However, because of the connection between deep layers and shallow ones established by shortcuts, the gradient can be directly transferred without any loss, which avoids gradient vanishing or explosion and accelerates learning process.

Third, it introduces multiscale receptive field. Now the input to every residual block combines features from different layers' output, which extracts features of different complexity from different length of input signals. This kind of multiscale learning corresponds to biological nature of human cognition.

3.2 Network Architecture

Based on the idea of residual learning discussed above, we construct a 1D CNN network shown in Fig. 1a. The whole architecture stacks residual blocks with different number of kernels. The basic structure of residual block is shown in Fig. 1b. It consists of two convolutional layers with batch-norm and relu activation, and adds a shortcut connection from the input to the output of the second layer. We have used the pre-activation version recommended in [14] which means stacking layers in relu-bn-conv style. The only variable of each residual block is the number of kernels.

The whole network starts with a first convolutional layer with 16 kernels. Then there are three stacked residual blocks with 16 kernels and a max pooling layer. Next, two stacked residual blocks with 32 kernels and another max pooling layer followed. After each pooling we have 1×1 convolutional layer to transform channels numbers for the convenience of shortcut connection because it is more difficult to realize if the channel number of input and output differs. Finally, we use global average pooling layer to unify the feature maps among all channels and a softmax layer to get the probability for each class. All the convolutional kernels are 1×3 in order to achieve more complicated model in small receptive field.

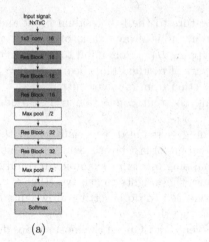
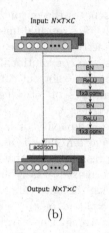

Fig. 1. (a) The structure of the whole network. N, T, C respectively represents number of input samples, time points and channels. (b) Detailed design inside every Res Block. The basic design follows [8]. The BN layer is prepositioned for better performance.

4   Saliency Map

A question well-worth researching in HAR is: where is the optimal position to place sensors? Answering this question could help us in i) abandoning irrelevant channels in order to achieve higher accuracy, ii) reducing the dimensions of the input signals and improve the efficiency of both training and inferring, and iii) reducing the obtrusiveness and hassle of wearing too many sensors which could affect normal daily life.

There have been many works trying to find the answer by wearing sensors on all potential positions, like the head, chest, upper arm, wrist, waist, thigh, leg and ankle [5,16]. Then they trained different networks with all combinations of sensors and compare the performances. The combination of sensors for model with the best performance is considered as the optimal position.

However, this approach has obvious problems. First, it requires an extensive research to train many different networks, which is time-consuming and cumbersome. The number of combinations will also explode when the possible positions increase. Second, the gaps between the best model and others are too small to judge. In the experiment of [5], the thigh was considered to be the best place with 99% accuracy. However, the model trained with sensors on chest and side waist also achieved 98.5% and 98.34% respectively. It is hard to tell if this gap is just because of noise or sensors on thigh is really better than other places.

Therefore, we use a method called *Saliency Map*. It is widely used in the image classification field to visualize which part of input image contributes most to the classification result. The core idea is to compute the gradient of classification unit to input signals, as Eq. 2 shows.

Fig. 2. Saliency Map for class Opendoor1. We computed Saliency Map for every sample in this class and averaged them all in order to eliminate the effect of noise. Each channel is associated with one sensor.

$$\omega = \frac{\partial S_c}{\partial I} \tag{2}$$

where S_c denotes the classification score for class c and I is the input signal. ω has the same dimensionality with input signal. It can be seen as the extent that how the scores will change along with input signal. From another perspective, it can also be considered as weights applied on inputs. If the weight is large, even small changes in input signal will result in big difference so we can say the result is sensitive to these channels and vice versa.

In practice, the dimensionality of the saliency map for a single sample is $T \times C$. T denotes the length of time series and C is number of channels. We add up the matrix along vertical axis because time length can not be treated separately. In the end, we obtain an array whose length is the same as the number of channels. If plotted, we can see peaks and valleys, like the ones in Fig. 2.

It is worth noting that a single sample has randomness, so the Saliency Map generated will be affected by noise. Therefore, a stable Saliency Map should be the average of abundant Saliency Maps generated by samples of the same class.

The values attached to each channel can be seen as the representation of importance. Therefore, we can consider channels with top values as the most important sensors. We have conducted more experiments in Sect. 5.5 to find out how convincing these top channels are and what kind of benefits it could bring.

5   Experiment and Result

This section includes the introduction of the dataset we used and several tests we conducted to prove the practicality of our theory.

5.1   Dataset

The OPPORTUNITY Activity Recognition Dataset is one of the most popular HAR datasets [3]. It originated from OPPORTUNITY challenge in 2010 and is still used as benchmark test of many state-of-the-art structures. Overall, it contains recordings of four subjects in a daily living scenario performing morning activities, with sensor-rich environment. We are focusing on Task B2 which contains 18 classes. During the recordings, each subject performed a session five times with activities of daily living (ADL) and one drill session. During each ADL session, subjects perform the activities without any restriction, by following a loose description of the overall actions to perform (i.e., checking ingredients and utensils in the kitchen, preparing and drinking a coffee, preparing and eating a sandwich, cleaning up). During the drill sessions, subjects performed 20 repetitions of a predefined sorted set of 17 activities. The dataset contains about 6 hours of recordings in total.

We follow the mainstream training and testing setting to make it possible to compare our work with famous and recent ones. It means training our network on all five ADL sessions and drill session for the first subject and on ADL1, ADL2 and drill sessions for Subjects 2 and 3, reporting classification performance on a testing set composed of ADL4 and ADL5 for Subjects 2 and 3. ADL3 sessions for Subjects 2 and 3 are left for validation.

In terms of the sensor setting, we follow the OPPORTUNITY challenge guidelines, taking into account only the on-body sensors. This includes 5 commercial RS485-networked XSense inertial measurement units (IMU) included in a custom-made motion jacket, 2 commercial InertiaCube3 inertial sensors located on each foot and 12 Bluetooth acceleration sensors on the limbs. Each IMU is composed of a 3D accelerometer, a 3D gyroscope and a 3D magnetic sensor, offering multimodal sensor information. Each sensor axis is treated as an individual channel, yielding an input space with a dimension of 113 channels. Since raw data is continuous 1-dimensional time series signal with multiple channels which is unable to be trained on, we have applied the data segmentation method recommended in [3]. The sample rate of these sensors is 30 Hz and recommended time window is 500 ms. It means each segmentation consists of 15 time points. In conclusion, the raw data is turned into training data with $N \times 15 \times 113$ dimensionality.

One main problem of the OPPORTUNITY dataset is its unbalanced distribution between different classes. For example, NULL class dominates the whole dataset with more than 80% but Open Drawer 1 - the minimum class, only occupies 1%. It has some risky disadvantages. The whole model will be very easily overfitting on small classes but is not showing any evidences since NULL class dominates the most. We will try to discuss and ease this unbalanced feature in Sect. 5.4.

5.2   Experiment Parameters

The whole network is trained on single MacBook Pro with 8 Intel Core i9 processors and AMD Radeon Pro 5000M. Our training uses mini-batch gradient

Table 1. Comparison of NF, parameters, and FLOPs of our ResNet-like structure and four baseline networks on OPPORTUNITY dataset. The metrics with a "*" mean they are not reported in the original paper and we do the computation by ourselves.

	NF	Parameters	FLOPs
Yang et al. 2015	85.1	0.912M*	1.85M*
Ordonez and Roggen, 2016	88.3	7.44M	54.58M*
Tang et al. 2020 baseline	86.1	3.2M	41.9M
Tang et al. 2020 simplified	84.5	0.42M	13.78M
Our ResNet-like structure	**89.2**	**0.024M**	**0.25M**

descent with 0.9 momentum and 256 batch size. The learning rate is set as 0.001 initially and divided by 10 when plateau. We have tested many other hyperparameters and ended up choosing this group that worked best. Since the selection of parameters is not the main topic of this work, we don't do more demonstration and discussion.

5.3   Performance

The results of our ResNet-like structure and four baseline networks on OPPORTUNITY dataset are shown in Table 1. We have chosen two most famous work [6, 26] and one most recent method [22]. Following [6], normalized F-measure(NF) is used to evaluate the performance.

From the comparison, we can see that our ResNet-like structure performs better than all four baselines with a significant reduction in parameters and FLOPs. Actually, there has already been a trend to explore more efficient networks while keeping the performance stable, reducing parameters by more than ten times. However, there is still a significant gap in computational complexity between our network and very recent work. We attribute this significant reduction to several factors. First, we found that most of the previous works treated the data format as 2-dimensional map and only did convolutions on time axis, leaving channels unchanged. It means keeping 113 channels throughout the whole network, which is obviously a burden. Like in [26], the first layer does 1×5 unpadded convolution to the input signals, changing it from $N \times 113 \times 30$ into $N \times 113 \times 26 \times 50$. However, in our network, we treat channels of sensors and 'channels' of kernels the same, which is very different from the mentioned method. Our first layer transforms input data from $N \times 15 \times 113$ into $N \times 15 \times 16$, which can be seen as the rearrangement of different sensors' signals. The different ways to treat two kinds of channels lead to the significant reduction of parameter numbers. Second, we got rid of the fully connected (FC) layers and use global average pooling [14] instead. FCs is notorious about the explosion of parameters and we find that a network without them for HAR, like in many other fields, can still achieve equivalent performance. Finally, the residual block makes learning easier as explained in Sect. 3.1, so that we can use very few kernels compared with

Table 2. Comparison between the same network trained with different setting of training dataset.

	Part with NULL	Part without NULL	Full with NULL	Full without NULL
Yang et al. 2015	89.2	77.3	93.7	90.1

previous works while achieving same performance. We use 16 and 32 kernels here which is significantly reduced from 128 [6], 60 [15] and 64 [22].

5.4   Discussion of Unbalance

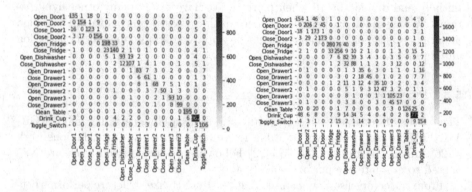

Fig. 3. Left: Confusion matrix of the network trained with full data. Right: Confusion matrix of the network trained with partial data

Besides comparing our network with state-of-the-art works in a mainstream training setting for OPPORTUNITY, we have conducted several more experiments with different setting. We remove NULL class to see more clearly what happens inside small classes. We also have tried training on the whole dataset with and without NULL class, applying train-val-test split by 8-1-1, to see if the increasing data will affect the performance of same model. The results are shown in Table 2. The confusion matrix for part without NULL and full without NULL is shown in Fig. 3 for more detailed discussion.

From the results, we can see that both in part dataset and full dataset, if NULL class is discarded, the performance drops at different level. This provides efficient evidence for the problem mentioned before: the unbalanced distribution of different classes in OPPORTUNITY. After discarding the dominant NULL class, the problem of lacking data for some small classes emerges. That is why the performance drops. We can also see that the network trained with full dataset has a relative small margin. That is because full dataset has more data which eases the overfitting problem, especially for some small classes.

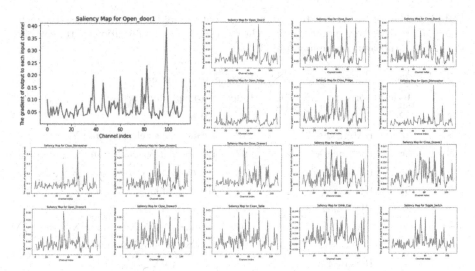

Fig. 4. Saliency Maps for all 17 activities in OPPORTUNITY, Open door1's is zoomed in for detailed observation and explanation.

When we conducted a parallel comparison between full and part dataset, the performance is improved by 4.5% when with NULL and 13% when without. It means obviously that providing more data can greatly enhance the network, especially when there is strong overfitting in original network. It also provides the evidence that current network structure is complex enough and what we need is to collect more data for improvement.

When it comes to the confusion matrix, we found that network trained with part dataset does not perform very well. Some samples will be misclassified as any class which means the network has not learnt an appropriate feature representation for the correct class. At the same time, the network trained with full dataset performs very well. The misclassification mainly happens in block diagonal matrix, which means the correct class and output class has just nuance. It means the network has learnt deep features but these features are not strong enough to classify between these very close classes. The possible improvement method should be more complicated network structure or new technical idea.

5.5 Saliency Map Usage

As discussed above, the Saliency Map for each activity class in OPPORTUNITY appears to be a curve with 113 points after processing. Each point is corresponding to one channel of a sensor and the value is considered to be the importance of this channel to the final result.

During experiments, we computed Saliency Map for every activity class and showed it in Fig. 4. First of all, let's take a look from big picture. Each map has clear peaks and valleys, which means we can easily extract channels with

Table 3. The top 10 and bottom 10 indexes from the saliency map for class 1 - open door1 and their corresponding sensors. The correspondence and positions of the sensors or other information can be found in [3].

Top 10 maximum		Bottom 10 minimum	
Index	Corresponding sensor	Index	Corresponding sensor
62	RLA mag X	15	LH acc Y
40	BACK acc Z	112	R-Shoe AngVelNavFrame Y
56	RLA acc X	97	L-Shoe AngVelNavFrame Y
55	RUA mag Z	108	R-Shoe AngVelNavFrame X
54	RUA mag Y	113	R-Shoe AngVelNavFrame Z
53	RUA mag X	75	LLA acc Y
44	BACK mag X	94	L-Shoe AngVelNavFrame X
84	L-Shoe Eu Y	96	L-Shoe AngVelNavFrame Y
99	R-Shoe Eu X	77	LLA gyro X
100	R-Shoe Eu Y	92	R-Shoe AngVelNavFrame X

Table 4. The same network structure with same learning schedule trained with different setting of input channels

How many channels used	Performance (NF)	Parameters in total
All 113	91.6	24594
Top 20	88.1	19650
Bottom 20	57.6	19650

high or low importance. Another interesting fact is that similar activities have similar patterns, particularly obvious are the map for Open Dishwasher and Close Dishwasher. It makes sense because in similar activities, such as opening or closing something, high importance should be given to same sensors, which is exactly what we have observed.

Then we take a step closer to analyze the information given by every single map. Because of the limited page length, we can not give each map a detailed explanation. Therefore, we mainly made detailed explanation for Activity 1: Open Door1, and other maps can be further explored in the same way.

To check if the values of each point has any realistic meaning, we cut out the top 10 channels with most importance and bottom 10 with least. The index numbers and corresponding sensors are shown in Table 3.

From Table 3, we can see that top 10 sensors mainly consist of sensors on right hand (RUA RLA) and on back (BACK), especially magnetic. It is reasonable since the key to opening the door is the movement of the right hand and the rotation of the waist. It doesn't matter what the left hand is doing or the state of the lower body. At the same time, there are some sensors about left hand in bottom 10 sensors which means signals related to left hands have little effect on classification, which is the same result as above. Besides, nearly all AngVelNavFrame sensors are on bottom 10 which means this kind of sensor is all useless for classification. AngVelNavFrame, according to its description in [3], represents orientation of the sensor with respect to a world coordinate system in quaternions. It is a useless feature beyond any doubts, because nobody cares which direction I'm heading when I open a door.

In order to further verify our theory, we average maps for every activity to generate the final Saliency Map for this whole dataset. Then we extract top 20 channels with highest values and bottom 20 channels as well. We have trained three different networks separately with all 113 channels, top 20 channels and bottom channels.

The results are shown in Table 4.

According to results, the performance of the whole model just drops by 3% when we choose top 20 channels as inputs instead of whole 113, while the parameters are reduced by 20%. It means that we must have discarded most useless channels and only the channels with strong ability to classify between different classes remain, significantly improving the efficiency of learning useful features.

At the same time, we observe that network trained with 20 top and 20 bottom have same network structure and same number of parameters but end up with totally different performance (88.1% and 57.6%). It provides the evidence of the assumption that channels with larger values on Saliency Map have stronger classification ability again.

It is worth noting that even the network trained with 20 bottom channels has stronger classification ability compared to empty model, which means there are still some information inside the channels which are discarded.

In conclusion, the values of Saliency Map can indeed reflect the importance of the corresponding sensor. Depending on the results of Saliency Map towards whole dataset, we can get direct feedback about which channels are most important. Therefore, dimensional reduction can be done by reserving channels with highest values and dropping the others. The optimal positions or sensors could also be found by directly comparing the values inside the Saliency Map.

6   Conclusion and Future Work

In this paper, we proposed a new ResNet-like CNN structure for HAR tasks. This novel network takes advantage of residual learning and achieves state-of-the-art performance with significant parameters and computational complexity reduction. The improvement can be attributed to three factors: i) a different processing method towards sensor channel and kernel channel, ii) removing fc layers, and iii) making kernel numbers smaller using residual learning. Another contribution of our work is the application of Saliency Map in HAR model. Using this method, we can visualize the importance of every input channel, which is corresponding to actual sensors wore on different positions. Based on the Saliency Map, we can visualize the importance of each sensor and conduct further work like dimension reduction to improve computational efficiency or find the optimal position with the largest value.

In our experiments, we demonstrated the performance of the proposed ResNet-like structure and compared it to other state-of-the-art works to prove its advantages. We also conducted a contrast test to show that the usage of Saliency Map can really benefit the network. Therefore, we believe that a ResNet-like structure can serve as a competitive structure of feature learning and classification for HAR problems and Saliency Map will serve as another useful tool.

For future work, there are two main ways to proceed. First, we will keep exploring the application of more advanced CNN network architecture on HAR tasks, like DenseNet, MobileNet, and others. Second, since the usefulness of Saliency Map is verified, a more complicated system should be designed to automatically realize the dimensional reduction work, like reserving the top 20 channels. We would also like to develop our novel network to specific applications of Physical Therapy to test the robustness on actual application scenarios.

References

1. Bordes, A., Glorot, X., Weston, J., Bengio, Y.: Joint learning of words and meaning representations for open-text semantic parsing. In: Artificial Intelligence and Statistics, pp. 127–135. PMLR (2012)
2. Bulling, A., Blanke, U., Schiele, B.: A tutorial on human activity recognition using body-worn inertial sensors. ACM Comput. Surv. (CSUR) **46**(3), 1–33 (2014)
3. Chavarriaga, R., et al.: The opportunity challenge: a benchmark database for on-body sensor-based activity recognition. Pattern Recogn. Lett. **34**(15), 2033–2042 (2013)
4. Chen, Y., Xue, Y.: A deep learning approach to human activity recognition based on single accelerometer. In: 2015 IEEE International Conference on Systems, Man, and Cybernetics, pp. 1488–1492. IEEE (2015)
5. Cleland, I., et al.: Optimal placement of accelerometers for the detection of everyday activities. Sensors (Basel) **13**(7), 9183–200 (2013). https://doi.org/10.3390/s130709183, https://www.ncbi.nlm.nih.gov/pubmed/23867744
6. Hammerla, N.Y., Halloran, S., Plötz, T.: Deep, convolutional, and recurrent models for human activity recognition using wearables. arXiv preprint arXiv:1604.08880 (2016)
7. Harrison, C., Tan, D., Morris, D.: Skinput: appropriating the body as an input surface. In: Proceedings of the SIGCHI Conference on Human Factors in Computing Systems, pp. 453–462 (2010)
8. He, K., Zhang, X., Ren, S., Sun, J.: Deep residual learning for image recognition. In: Proceedings of the IEEE Conference on Computer Vision and Pattern Recognition, pp. 770–778 (2016)
9. Hinton, G., et al.: Deep neural networks for acoustic modeling in speech recognition: the shared views of four research groups. IEEE Signal Process. Mag. **29**(6), 82–97 (2012)
10. Howard, A.G., et al.: MobileNets: efficient convolutional neural networks for mobile vision applications. arXiv preprint arXiv:1704.04861 (2017)
11. Huang, G., Liu, Z., Van Der Maaten, L., Weinberger, K.Q.: Densely connected convolutional networks. In: Proceedings of the IEEE Conference on Computer Vision and Pattern Recognition, pp. 4700–4708 (2017)

12. Krizhevsky, A., Sutskever, I., Hinton, G.E.: ImageNet classification with deep convolutional neural networks. In: Advances in Neural Information Processing Systems, pp. 1097–1105

13. LeCun, Y., Bengio, Y., Hinton, G.: Deep learning. Nature **521**(7553), 436–444 (2015)

14. Lin, M., Chen, Q., Yan, S.: Network in network. arXiv preprint arXiv:1312.4400 (2013)

15. Ordóñez, F.J., Roggen, D.: Deep convolutional and LSTM recurrent neural networks for multimodal wearable activity recognition. Sensors **16**(1), 115 (2016)

16. Pannurat, N., Thiemjarus, S., Nantajeewarawat, E., Anantavrasilp, I.: Analysis of optimal sensor positions for activity classification and application on a different data collection scenario. Sensors (Basel) **17**(4) (2017). https://doi.org/10.3390/s17040774, https://www.ncbi.nlm.nih.gov/pubmed/28379208

17. Pourbabaee, B., Roshtkhari, M.J., Khorasani, K.: Deep convolutional neural networks and learning ECG features for screening paroxysmal atrial fibrillation patients. IEEE Trans. Syst. Man Cybern. Syst. **48**(12), 2095–2104 (2018)

18. Qin, J., Liu, L., Zhang, Z., Wang, Y., Shao, L.: Compressive sequential learning for action similarity labeling. IEEE Trans. Image Process. **25**(2), 756–769 (2015)

19. Simonyan, K., Vedaldi, A., Zisserman, A.: Deep inside convolutional networks: visualising image classification models and saliency maps. arXiv preprint arXiv:1312.6034 (2013)

20. Simonyan, K., Zisserman, A.: Very deep convolutional networks for large-scale image recognition. In: ICLR (2014)

21. Szegedy, C., et al.: Going deeper with convolutions. In: Proceedings of the IEEE Conference on Computer Vision and Pattern Recognition, pp. 1–9 (2015)

22. Tang, Y., Teng, Q., Zhang, L., Min, F., He, J.: Efficient convolutional neural networks with smaller filters for human activity recognition using wearable sensors. arXiv preprint arXiv:2005.03948 (2020)

23. Vepakomma, P., De, D., Das, S.K., Bhansali, S.: A-wristocracy: Deep learning on wrist-worn sensing for recognition of user complex activities. In: 2015 IEEE 12th International Conference on Wearable and Implantable Body Sensor Networks (BSN), pp. 1–6. IEEE (2015)

24. Wang, J., Chen, Y., Hao, S., Peng, X., Hu, L.: Deep learning for sensor-based activity recognition: a survey. Pattern Recogn. Lett. **119**, 3–11 (2019)

25. Xia, K., Huang, J., Wang, H.: LSTM-CNN architecture for human activity recognition. IEEE Access **8**, 56855–56866 (2020)

26. Yang, J., Nguyen, M.N., San, P.P., Li, X.L., Krishnaswamy, S.: Deep convolutional neural networks on multichannel time series for human activity recognition. In: Twenty-Fourth International Joint Conference on Artificial Intelligence (2015)

27. Zeng, M., et al.: Convolutional neural networks for human activity recognition using mobile sensors. In: 6th International Conference on Mobile Computing, Applications and Services, pp. 197–205. IEEE (2014)

Author Index

Printed in the United States
by Baker & Taylor Publisher Services